The Infinite Tarot

*The Essential Guide
for Connecting to the All-Knowing Source*

By

Sheilaa Hite, C.Ht, C.L.C., M.I.A.

©2017

Copyright ©2017 by Sheilaa Hite

All rights reserved. No part of this book, either in part or in whole, may be reproduced, transmitted, utilized in any manner or by any means—graphic, electronic, photographic or mechanical, including photocopying, mimeographing, recording, taping or by any information storage and retrieval system, without the prior written permission of the Publisher, excepting brief quotes used in connection with reviews and articles.

Author's photo by Stephanie Stanton,
www.stephaniestantonphotography.com

The Tarot cards used in this book are from the
Original Rider-Waite deck, now in the public domain.

Printed in the United States of America

ISBN 978-0-9916-5533-5

The Center for Practical Spirituality
P.O. Box 472
Lenox, MA 01240 USA

www.SheilaaHite.com

Table of Contents

Acknowledgements

Introduction 1

Chapter 1 7
Where Did the Tarot Originate?

Chapter 2 11
What is the Tarot?
What Can the Tarot Be Used For?

Chapter 3 15
Choosing Your Deck

Chapter 4 19
The Care and Handling of Your Tarot Deck

Chapter 5 23
Reverse Cards, Falling Cards, Significators, Shuffling, Expiration Dates and Recommended Reading

Chapter 6 33
Liberating Terminology, Color Symbology, Numerology

A Professional Intuitive's Perspective on The Fool 41

Chapter 7 43
The Major Arcana

Chapter 8 95
The Minor Arcana, Suits, Numbered Cards, Court Cards

Chapter 9 193
How to Conduct a Tarot Consultation
How to Phrase Questions During a Tarot Consultation
Timing of Events During a Tarot Consultation
Tarot, Past Lives and Karma
What to Do When You Draw A Blank
Getting to Know Your Tarot Cards
Exercise 1 – Know Thyself: Best and Least Liked Cards
My Life Path and Life Guidance Tarot Cards
Reading the Cards
Working With the Cards
Keeping It Simple
Clarifying Cards
Your Mission
Integrity
Reading the Tarot for Yourself

Chapter 10 233
Tarot Spreads and Charts
1-Card Reading
3-Card Reading (Linear)
Chalice Spread
Dream Interpretation
Personal Power Spread
I Am Spread
Relationship Spread
The Process Spread
Defining Moment Spread
Crossroads Spread
The Tower Spread
Ripples in a Pond Spread
Money Bags Spread
Spiral Revelations Spread
Painting the Sistine Chapel Spread
What Is My Life's Purpose? Spread
My Karma Spread
Karma Crossroads Spread

About the Author 277

*I dedicate this book to
Cassandra Saulter, who gave me my first Tarot deck
and Alexandra Summer, who introduced me to the original Mythic Tarot deck*

Guided Tarot Meditations

Guided meditations are great for helping you access your inner consciousness. My guided meditations will help you establish and maintain a relationship with the cards, characters and information sources of the Tarot.

With the purchase of The Infinite Tarot guide, you also receive access to a free download of two of my Tarot guided meditations. Just go to my website—www.SheilaaHite.com and click on 'Store' and scroll down to 'Free Tarot Meditations Download' and click on that.

Acknowledgements

Every person has the potential to contribute to life in a meaningful way. They can't do it alone, though. In addition to having a desire to contribute, they must also have positive reflections of their value, encouraging people around them, an expectation from others that they will manifest their potential, an accumulation of necessary knowledge, skills, talents and gifts and the Divine spark of inspiration.

Without the Divine spark from the "Front Office", and the support of my students and friends in my Advanced Tarot workshop—Linda Farmer, Robin Hare, Louise Rossi-Edwards, Ralston Edwards, Winslow Eliot and Ginny Guenette, this book might still be on my "to do" list.

They are the positive, encouraging, generous mirrors of my value and my commitment to fully engage with life and I am grateful.

A special thanks to Linda Farmer for contributing her own insightful tarot spreads and for designing the format of the spreads in this book and to Winslow Eliot for her wisdom and generosity as she edited the manuscript.

Many thanks to the phenomenal Tim Moriarty and his staff at Square One Design and the talented Angela Flores of Paisley Prints, Etc. for working their magic and turning my assemblage of words and illustrations into a cohesive and lovely reality.

I'm happy to express my gratitude for my dear friends, David Nathan for his belief in me and James Wecker II for expecting only the

Acknowledgements

best from me.

A most appreciative thank you to Tarot maven Mary K. Greer whose ground breaking workbook, "Tarot for Yourself", did so much to enhance and expand my Tarot comfort level, as well as enrich my knowledge and understanding of this great Intuitive tool.

In this and all versions of my work and all areas of my life, I thank my guardian angel, my maternal grandmother, Lois, with all my heart. I love you and thank you for helping me to see myself as being as beautiful as you see me. And always and forever, I thank you for watching over me, I feel your love and your wings around me always.

Introduction

The Tarot is a fascinating, record-keeping personal GPS system consisting of 78 cards that can help guide you in answering important questions and making your dreams come true.

My relationship with the Tarot deck and its 78 cards is a personal, intuitive one. The cards speak to me and I have learned to listen to them and trust what they tell me. In the process of learning to establish a relationship with the cards, I've learned so much more about myself, others and life.

Because of my intuitive relationship with the Tarot, my accuracy rate is 95-100%, and I've been told by clients and students alike that my ability to interpret the cards is legendary.

When you read the Table of Contents of almost any Tarot instruction book, you'll notice that the books are pretty much laid out the same way—facts about the Tarot, the Tarot cards and sample lay-outs, spreads and readings.

The Infinite Tarot guide is different than the others. True, it's laid out the same as the other books, however, unlike those other books, its content and purpose are different and it's more than just facts, words and card lay-outs. The purpose of this guide is to give you a clearer, more powerful access to and understanding of the Tarot and yourself as well as your natural gift of intuition because it teaches you how to develop a more personal, intuitive relationship with the Tarot cards.

Introduction

As an Intuitive Consultant, I've learned that I can clearly see all aspects of my client's issues and find previously hidden solutions to their most vexing problems. As a teacher, I've learned that I can show others how to find and develop their own very accurate, powerful relationship with the Tarot and themselves.

Though born with the gift of active intuition, my professional metaphysical journey began with Astrology. I never intended to learn the Tarot, in fact, the only interest I had in it was when I consulted someone else for a reading. I thought that learning 78 cards and their meanings would be too difficult and I didn't mind explaining this to others whenever they suggested I should study this system. That didn't stop them from insisting that I'd be good at it and giving me their Tarot decks because I was so good at interpreting an Astrology chart.

One day, a Numerologist friend whom I'd introduced to Astrology, called to tell me that she'd just bought a deck of Tarot cards co-designed by my favorite Astrologer, Liz Greene. The deck was called, The Mythic Tarot, and she sounded very excited. Since she felt the same way I did about learning the Tarot, I was intrigued to hear the tale of her 'Tarot seduction.'

We met the next afternoon and she showed me her new toy, The Mythic Tarot deck. Seeing that it was based on Greek mythology and knowing that it was co-created by Liz Greene, I was immediately smitten. I called the Bodhi Tree bookstore (I was living in West Hollywood at the time) and had them reserve a copy of the deck for me.

After our meeting, I raced to the Bodhi Tree and made what turned out to be a life-changing purchase. I knew I had to find teachers and take classes before I could begin to study, memorize and interpret the cards. Tired though I was from a long and busy day, as I prepared for

Introduction

bed that night, I remembered to make a note to call the Philosophical Research Society the following day and inquire about their classes.

You're familiar with the saying, "Man plans and God laughs," aren't you? Well, God must have been rolling in the aisles when I made my plans to find teachers and study the Tarot because it didn't go that way at all.

At about three o'clock in the morning, I was awakened by my Spirit Guides who told me that they would be teaching me the Tarot. They explained that they'd wake me every morning at three o'clock for lessons, meditations and channelings that would reveal all I needed to know in order to master this ancient art. Honored and excited, I thanked them and told them I looked forward to working with them the following morning. Considering the matter settled, I tried to get back to sleep.

They weren't having any of that, though. They very kindly but firmly told me that they'd been waiting patiently for me to find this Tarot deck and now that I had, the lessons would begin that very morning. I wanted to go back to sleep and I can be as stubborn as any two-year old, so I told them that they could do what they wanted but I was going to sleep and we could start my lessons in 24 hours. They acknowledged that I had free will and didn't have to begin the lessons until I wanted to. They also acknowledged that they had a job to do, and while they wouldn't interfere with any of my other plans, I wouldn't be sleeping again until I started taking the lessons!

As I stated before, I can be stubborn. I refused to start the lessons and they refused to let me sleep—not even a nap! I held out for two days. Finally, exhausted, I surrendered. The lessons began that morning and continued for two months. Those sessions were some of the most enlightening, electrifying learning experiences of my life.

Introduction

When my Guides announced that the lessons had come to an end and I was ready to take my gift out into the world, I was both thrilled and sad. I'd come to love the time I spent with them as well as the wealth of knowledge they'd revealed to me. We said our good-byes and for the first time in two months, I got to sleep before dawn.

The next day my phone rang and when I answered it, I was surprised to hear the voice of a friend I hadn't heard from in years. She told me that she'd found my phone number in some old papers and had decided to give me a call. I thought that was odd because I'd moved several times since we'd last communicated and there was no way she could have my current number.

She asked what I'd been up to and, when I told her about completing my spiritually directed Tarot course, she insisted that I give her a reading right then and there. I began to beg off, explaining that I'd just finished my training and had never done a Tarot card reading for anyone. That's when she did the most curious thing—her voice changed so much that it didn't sound like her at all and she said with great authority, "Of course you can read the cards. Now read them!"

So I read the cards for her. I answered her questions, all the while feeling nervous and self-conscious. When I was finished, still speaking with that authoritative voice, she told me, "You did very well. Never doubt that you have a gift. Take it out into the world and continue to nurture it." And then her voice changed back into that light, girlish tone that I'd always known her to use and we talked about all of the things that old friends talk about when they've had a long absence from each other.

When we hung up, I knew then as I know now that my friend's 'out of the blue' phone call wasn't a social call from a long lost friend, it was a test and a graduation ceremony. However Divine Guidance

Introduction

works, it had conspired for me to be able to relate to a Tarot deck, to receive teachings from on High, to immediately experience sharing my gift with another and to receive a celestial "Atta girl!" for my efforts.

Because I didn't get my initial training from books or corporeal teachers, I didn't learn that certain suits or cards are considered 'bad', 'weak', 'good' or 'strong'. I learned to accept all of them, to observe them and to listen to them as they presented themselves to me at the time that a question is asked or an issue is raised. I learned that they'll always reflect the energy of the seeker, the situation and the question.

Because I learned this way, and because it works, I teach this way. My students find and nurture their own inner greatness just as I did with my Guides. They better understand themselves, life and the Tarot through becoming conscious of their own mastery as they study with me.

And that is what I offer you in The Infinite Tarot, entre into a new World vision filled with infinite opportunities to encounter, develop and live in the light of your own greatness through studying the Tarot with me. So, welcome, pull up a chair, put your cards on the table and let's begin!

— 1 —
Where Did the Tarot Originate?

The truth is, no one is really certain. There are many stories about this venerable oracle and its origins. As with so many historical events and discoveries, the real truth has gotten lost and/or mixed up with other bits and pieces of history. A person could spend years researching and amassing all of the 'data' regarding the history of the Tarot and still not be able to accurately pin-point its beginnings.

Each practitioner tells the version of the story they like best and most of them believe it and swear to its accuracy. I have a favorite, as well. Whether it's true or not, I can't tell you. It makes as much sense to me as the other stories do to their advocates.

Why am I so blasé about the origins of a subject that I'm so enlightened and inspired by? Because the Tarot is somehow different from the other Intuitive Arts. It doesn't need its history to give it a patina of authenticity and accuracy. The Tarot, like any living organism, is 'alive' and proves itself and its valuable contribution to us with each turn of the cards. As we grow and evolve, so does the Tarot and our understanding of it.

Would I like to know where it really comes from, who really invented-created it, its journey to today's times told in its own words? Sure, I would. So much so, in fact, that I spent a lot of time researching and following up each lead I came across as I tried to solve the "great mystery" of the Tarot's genesis.

I was deep into my search when one day, it dawned on me, no

Where Did The Tarot Originate?

matter what its history is or how it came into our conscious awareness, that is not what really matters with the Tarot. I realized that, very often, Tarot researchers, myself included, lost sight of what was really important. We were too much in our heads as we spent so much energy on ferreting out the minutia about the Tarot and its origins that we were losing our spiritual, intuitive connection to the very heart and soul of it. We were like the farmer who owned the goose who laid a golden egg every day. Curious about how the goose produced the valuable golden egg, he cut her open, hoping to find out exactly how she produced such immense value on a daily basis. Good scientific process. Not very practical, though. Although he was able to see how the process worked, by dissecting the goose, he killed the living source that produced such infinite value.

Not wanting to 'kill the golden goose' and end its generous contribution to my life, I decided that I had studied the Tarot's origins enough. If I wanted a much more personal, powerful, intuitive relationship with the Tarot, I needed to lead with my heart and soul and not my head.

So, I decided to enjoy all of the different versions of the Tarot's beginnings and from them, I chose one that I liked the most and that's the one I tell people when they ask, "Where does the Tarot come from?"

"At one time in our history, the ancient city of Alexandria, Egypt was the greatest seat of knowledge, both esoteric and exoteric, on Earth. The greatest scholars, wisdom keepers and libraries were there and knowledge was revered, gathered and protected. The great scholars and wisdom keepers knew that in order for humanity to progress, we needed access to the information about our spiritual, mental, emotional and physical evolutions through all time.

For hundreds of years, the library flourished. As time went on, though, the wisdom keepers noticed that armies from civilizations that didn't revere knowledge as they did, were conquering lands closer and closer to Alexandria. They realized that it was just a matter of time before those conquering armies would be at the city's gates. Knowing that the library's most important volumes of information, those containing esoteric knowledge, were the most vulnerable, they devised a plan to protect and save the information contained within them.

They gathered their most powerful mystics and their finest artists and they transcribed the keys to the esoteric wisdom of the ages onto seventy-eight lambskins. They made several identical sets of the lambskins and paid the foreign merchants who traveled by caravan through their land to smuggle them out of the country past the armies of their enemies and into the hands of the wisdom keepers in other countries.

These foreign merchants distributed most of the sets of seventy-eight keys to various wisdom keepers in Europe, while keeping some of the esoteric sets of keys for themselves.

Over time, as each set was passed from person to person, they were copied and the images were added to or changed in some way that reflected the beliefs or perspectives of the person who had possession of them. Although the images were no longer identical to the original set, they each still contained the one thing that kept all of the sets true to the mission of the Library's scholars—they all still retained the core essence of the ancient truths that could evoke or reflect that truth in the heart and mind of the viewer.

Eventually, with the advent of the printing press, smaller paper copies of the original lambskins wound up in the hands of the wealthy in Europe as well as in the hands of the working class. Though the Tarot cards were used to play card games by all classes, a large percentage of both the working class and nobility used them as they'd been intended, to divine the esoteric secrets or mysteries. In so doing, both classes established a direct, personal connection to their spiritual guidance, eliminating the need to have the priests of the Church act as their emissaries to God.

Church attendance began to dwindle and so did the revenue the Church earned from the former parishioner's donations and tithes. The Church, in an effort to avert a financial crisis, mounted an intense campaign to woo their ex-parishioners back by declaring the cards and images the work of the devil and threatening that anyone caught using them would be excommunicated and forever burn in hell. They backed up their threats with physical force and legal manipulations and eventually the harassed and frightened parishioners returned to the fold.

Under the threat of pain, death and eternal damnation, the working class publically swore off using the oracle, but many of them continued to use it in secret. They formed underground groups and societies that kept the oracle in circulation and each group continued to add to and change the images while leaving the basic esoteric meanings intact.

In the late 19th century, a few esoteric groups in Europe courageously risked the wrath of the Church and publically espoused and encouraged the use of the cards for spiritual and mystical work. In December 1909, two members of The British group, the Hermetic Order of the Golden Dawn, Arthur Edward Waite and artist, Pamela Coleman Smith, created the Rider-Waite Smith Tarot deck. This was the first deck to use scenes instead of symbols for the numbered cards of the four suits of the Minor Arcana. It's considered the first modern Tarot deck and is still the most widely sold Tarot deck in the Western world.

From then on, the Tarot gradually became more and more accepted by the public and there are now thousands of published Tarot decks of diverse designs, as well as countless numbers of decks created by Tarot devotees for their own use."

— 2 —
What Is the Tarot?

The Tarot is a 78 card information retrieval system, a fascinating, record keeping personal GPS system that can help guide you in answering important questions and making your dreams come true. It operates by presenting a set of images to the conscious mind that evoke or stimulate a connection to subconscious, previously hidden knowledge. The images of the Tarot are basically a pictorial representation of all we, as sentient beings, know.

Because the conscious mind responds to words and the subconscious mind responds to symbols and images, we are naturally geared to experience more profound connections with the deeper parts of our consciousness via images, symbols and pictures. Once stimulated, the conscious mind is able to translate into words the meanings of the images our subconscious mind has shown us.

There is no "good" or "bad" or "strong" or "weak" card (although, there may be cards you like and don't like). The Tarot cards are meant to be neutral, to reflect archetypal images and energy. They take on or reflect the archetypal truth of the moment, issue, question, circumstance or person.

Archetypes are the original blueprints from which all things of the same kind are based. They are images, unconscious ideas or patterns of thought that are present in every person's subconscious.

All of the archetypes that the Tarot connects with dwell in the repository of the memory banks of all humanity. All cultures have their own mythology, their own archetypal treasury. All mythologies are related to each other, from the gods on Mount Olympus to the deities of the Yoruba religion to the Hindu saints, all of these archetypal symbols and energies are related and therefore, their information is accessible to and retrievable by all of us.

Whenever the archetypal 'account' is activated by connecting with the proper stimulus, it always yields a truth reflecting the stimulus and the energy of the moment. These are the moments that compel the Tarot to retrieve previously inaccessible information and 'speak' to us, revealing the answers to the questions we're asking.

What Can the Tarot Be Used For?

The Tarot is meant to enlighten us. The definitions of enlighten are **1-** *"to give greater knowledge and understanding about a subject or situation"* and **2-** *"to give spiritual knowledge or insight."*

Does that mean that you can only use it to ask about spiritual or philosophical ideas or issues?

Not in my Universe. You can use the Tarot to enlighten yourself about all manner of subjects, from the loftiest of matters to the most mundane of issues. Remember, it's an information retrieval system. It really doesn't care what you're asking about, its purpose is to help you get the information you're seeking.

There are Tarot practitioners who don't see it that way. They consider it a form of near blasphemy to use the oracle for anything as mundane as choosing which movie you're going to see. They've placed the Tarot and themselves on a pedestal and they look down upon

What Can the Tarot Be Used For?

anyone who uses the oracle in any way that they've decided is frivolous.

The Tarot is a powerful tool; the definition of tool is *"a device or implement used to carry out a particular function."* It's an aid meant to help you better understand yourself, your world and the people in it. You decide how you want to interact with and use this tool.

I use and interact with the Tarot in many, many ways. Some of them are:

1. As a mirror, to follow the dictum carved on ancient Greek temples, *"Know Thyself."* I ask it questions that will reveal to me a better and deeper understanding of myself, my motives, my path, my purpose.
2. As confirmation, often I've already come to a conclusion about something when I consult the cards and I want additional information.
3. As a tie breaker, to help me decide between two or more courses of action, processes, routes, movies, events, purchases, etc.
4. As a sleuth, to help me find the answers to the great mysteries of life, including, where I left my car keys.
5. As inspiration, to help me connect with my creative center.
6. As a meditation guide, to focus on the card pulled and 'follow' its lead as I meditate on the message its bringing me.
7. Connecting to Spirit, need I say more?
8. As a dear friend whom I know will always tell me the truth, whether I want to hear it or not.

Beginning with Carl Jung, many psychologists use the Tarot to help themselves and their patients successfully navigate the road of life. It's an excellent tool for delving into and deciphering the motivations for our actions, as well as assisting us in developing healthy new life habits.

What Can the Tarot Be Used For?

I have a friend who's a sports fan. She uses the oracle to help her choose the winning team in any contest; she's pretty good at it, too. (I tried that a few times and was a dismal failure at it. Now, I find out the winner the old-fashioned way, I await the outcome of the game.)

The point is, this marvelous oracle is a gift that was given to us in order to help us access information so that we can live our lives as we were intended, with grace, courage, faith, audacity, love, hope and joy.

— 3 —
Choosing Your Tarot Deck

Choosing your Tarot deck is a very special and uncomplicated process, although you wouldn't know that from some of the set-in-concrete 'advice' given by many Tarot practitioners and teachers. Prospective students ask me about the veracity of this kind of 'advice' all the time. Here is a sample of some of those so called "pearls of wisdom":

1. ***Never*** buy your first deck, it ***must*** be given to you as a gift.
2. ***Always*** purchase your first deck yourself, only you can choose the cards you'll work with.
3. No matter how many decks you have, ***never*** accept a deck from someone as a gift.
4. Your first deck ***must*** be given to you by an experienced Tarot practitioner.
5. ***Never*** accept a deck that's been used by someone else.
6. Money ***cannot*** be exchanged for your first deck, it demeans the oracle.
7. Money ***must*** be exchanged for your first deck, it signifies the strength of your commitment to the Tarot.

Pretty confusing, huh? I could go on, but I think you're getting my point. Those 'always' and 'never' admonitions (unfortunately, there are many, many more like them) are based on the dogma that comes from trying to control any process that operates best when its allowed to freely flow and inform you in the way that works best for/with both you and the process. The 'always' and 'never' dogma rears its ugly head in many areas of our lives—spirituality, creativity, religion and anyplace else that people need to be free enough to make their own personal choices.

Dogma, like concrete, doesn't move or expand to fit the evolving truth that exists in each moment. I'm sure that it, like concrete, has its uses in our world. Not with the Tarot or any of the other Intuitive Arts, though.

Whenever someone tries to impose their dogma on me, I am immediately wary. Unknowingly, they're telling me that they're stuck in a limiting belief system. Most people don't even realize that they're stuck. For whatever reason, they allowed the limiting dogma to take hold and they never questioned themselves enough to find out if the belief system held any meaningful validity for them.

Why all of this when you just want to know about choosing a deck of Tarot cards?

The Tarot works with you on an intuitive level, always seeking the depths of your infinite repository of knowledge. Being able to hear and allow yourself to listen to your inner voice as you choose (and are chosen by) the particular 'vehicle', your deck, that will transport you to your repository is a requisite for aligning your spirit with the Source of Knowledge.

So, whether it's a gift from someone else, whoever they may be in your life, or a purchase you made for yourself, the most important things to keep in mind when you choose your first (and any other) deck are: **1-** *"Does it appeal to me visually?"* and **2-** *"How do I feel when I hold it in my hands?"*

We're a visual species and the Tarot is a set of images and symbols that we first consciously encounter with our eyes. If you don't like the way a deck looks, don't bother with how it'll feel when you hold it. If you do like the way it looks, hold it in your right hand, bring it up to your chest and hold it over your heart. Close your eyes and take several deep, rhythmic, gentle breaths. And notice how you feel when you to that. Do you feel at peace, agitated, happy, sad? Is your heart calm or is it racing? What thoughts are going through your mind?

If you feel agitated or sad or you feel nothing at all, you're obviously not holding the deck that's meant for you. If your heart is racing, is it from excitement or trepidation? If it's from trepidation—that isn't your deck, either. If negative or self-deprecating thoughts are going through your mind, that's what working with that particular deck will bring you, put it back on the shelf.

If you feel at peace, calm, happy and/or positive thoughts are going through your mind, you've found your Tarot deck.

Suppose, in your search for your first deck, you find more than one deck that feels good? You simply start the process all over again with the 'feel good' decks. One of them will give you a clear indication that the two of you are ready for (to paraphrase the last line in the classic film, *Casablanca*), *"The beginning of a beautiful friendship."*

What if, after you choose your first deck and begin working with it, you become attracted to another Tarot deck? Tarot decks are amazingly tolerant and won't be the least bit jealous if you bring a new deck into the 'family.' I currently work with seven Tarot decks. I let them 'tell' me which ones are to be used during a reading. (They 'tell' me energetically. I set them on a table and slowly move my right hand a few inches above them until I feel a strong energy pull to the correct deck.)

*** **NOTE:** It's considered a very high honor if an experienced Tarot practitioner passes one of their decks on to you. It means that Spirit is consciously acknowledging that you're ready to begin your Tarot journey.

— 4 —
The Care and Handling of Your Tarot Deck

It's important that you establish a relationship with your cards. However you obtain your cards, before you use them, you do need to 'clear' them of old energy. This process removes all of the old energetic imprints of all of the people the deck has interacted with on its way to you. Its energy 'slate' will then be blank, giving you the space to imprint your own energy patterns on it.

There are many ways to 'clear' a Tarot deck of old energy. One of the simplest and best ways is to shuffle the deck at least three times, while silently or out loud introducing yourself to it. Thank it for coming in to your life to help you on your path. Another way is to place the deck on a table, fan or spread the cards out and slowly wave a lit incense stick or sage bundle back and forth over them while introducing yourself and expressing gratitude for its having come into your life. Do this with the cards face up and again with the cards face down. Keep it simple and sincere and you'll create a lasting bond with your new cards in no time!

If your deck was given to you by someone who had used it and you want to have their energy with the deck along with yours, that's simple, as you introduce yourself to the deck, invite the person's energy to stay with the cards and help you as you work with the Tarot cards.

The 78 Tarot cards in the deck are your friends and allies who will always tell you the truth, be ceaselessly supportive and never judge

The Care and Handling of Your Tarot Deck

you. They will assist you in discovering and developing the unlimited "well-spring" of your inner knowledge, your intuition, as they inform and enlighten you.

Please remember, treat them the way you want to be treated, with care and respect. More than just pictures on paper, they represent sacred images that are a reflection of all of us as we experience the infinite play of life. As such, they profoundly mirror our desires, our needs, our conflicts and our aspirations, as well as act as guides who will direct us to the information and energy we need in order to live a life filled with meaning and satisfaction.

How you keep your Tarot cards is much more important than where you keep them or what you keep them in. Your relationship with the cards (as is your relationship with people, pets, plants and possessions) is determined by the type of energy and feeling you put into it. There are too many 'rules' regarding this aspect of forming and maintaining your relationship with your Tarot deck. These 'rules' limit and stifle the natural spark and flow of spontaneity necessary to you as you embark on one of the most rewarding adventures of your life. These 'rules' and their heavy, sluggish energy add up to more dogma.

Dogma lurks everywhere, just waiting for an opportunity to pounce and stifle the natural flow of energy of spirit, creativity and connection. Here too, it shows up to impose its stagnating will. A few examples of some of the 'rules' others have told me regarding the 'only' way to store your Tarot deck when you're not using it.

1. **Always** keep your Tarot cards in a box, the box helps to keep the energy of the cards connected to each other.
2. **Never** keep your Tarot cards in a box, the confined space of the box restricts the energy of the cards.
3. **Always** keep your Tarot cards wrapped in a silk cloth, silk is a

natural fiber produced by a living being and therefore conducts life energy.
4. **Never** keep your Tarot cards wrapped in a silk cloth, silk is a natural fiber produced by a living being whose energy contaminates the energy of your cards.

Of course, dogma being dogma, there are lots more *'always'* and *'nevers'*, about the kind of box; the shape of the box; the color of the cloth; the way the cards should or should not be placed, stored or wrapped. Exhausting isn't it?

The most important thing to know here is this, keep your Tarot deck in a special way and a special place. **Special means what is special to you**, not someone else's definition of what is special. If you want to keep them in a box, it doesn't matter what material the box is made of, as long as it pleases you. If you want to wrap them in a cloth, it doesn't matter what color the cloth is or what the cloth is made of, as long as it pleases you. If at any time you want to change the cloth and/or the container you keep your Tarot cards in, do so. What really matters is that your Tarot cards are kept together and are safe from dust and dirt.

A few years ago, a new student joined my class after having been in another beginner class. She'd become very confused and upset after having been admonished by her former teacher and several of her classmates for wanting to wrap her cards in a four inch strip of antique fabric and lace instead of the 'only' way her teacher insisted on.

She explained that she'd always been close to her grandmother, who had recently died. Her grandmother had been quite a beauty and very social when she was younger and had kept several of her beautiful old ball gowns. After her grandmother's death, the student had taken her grandmother's favorite ball gown and cut the antique fabric and lace trim from the hem of the garment and wrapped her cards with it.

The Care and Handling of Your Tarot Deck

She was able to still feel close to her grandmother and felt that her grandmother was helping her as she worked with the cards. When she told me her story, tears welled up in my eyes—what a wonderful way to keep and honor that that is most precious to you!

I'm just sorry the other teacher and her students were so numbed and blinded by dogma that they couldn't feel and see the grace, beauty and love that was present in that student's experience.

Handling your Tarot deck in a special way helps you to establish and maintain a relationship or ritual with them. Ritual—rite or celebration—is important to all of us because it focuses our senses and helps align our intuition and our minds so that we can be in attunement with Spirit. It's a lot like putting an appliance plug into an electrical outlet, once connected, we can open up to the source of information and the source of information can open up to us, thus providing us with conscious access to all of the information the cards were created to provide us with.

— 5 —
Reverse Cards, Falling Cards, Significators, Shuffling, Expiration Dates and Recommended Reading

Many Tarot practitioners interpret a Tarot card differently when it's upside down after it's been turned over by the Tarot practitioner or the querent. They feel that it's upside down to warn them that they need to pay special attention to the card.

What do I do when a reverse card shows up in a spread? I turn it right side up and I keep reading, interpreting the card from its now upright position.

I don't read reverse cards any differently than I do when they're upright. I've never had the experience (or the luck!) of walking into a room and seeing someone or something standing on their head so that I'd know I needed to pay special attention to them or be wary of them for some reason. I've always had to read the energy of a person, space or situation just the way it showed up, and I'm guessing that you've had to size up life's situations that way, too.

Inherent in each Tarot card are all of its possibilities—positive, negative and neutral. A card, regardless of its position, upright or upside down, the other cards around it and the energy of the question and the querent at the time of the reading contain more than enough information to attract your attention and guide you to all of the pertinent information related to the question or issue. It's been my

Falling Cards

experience that you can get all of the information you need from the cards in their upright position without adding the extra work and using the valuable time it takes to learn the reverse meanings of the cards.

I urge my students to learn to read the cards without placing special emphasis on reversed cards. If they've had prior experience reading the Tarot with reversed cards, I honor their experience and their method and I ask them not to read the cards from a reversed position during the class. Sometimes, a student who learned the Tarot with me will decide later that they want to read reverse cards and sometimes, a student with prior experience, will choose not to read reverse cards anymore. When that happens, I honor that person's choice and I encourage them to do what works best for them

That being said, when I consult with another Tarot card practitioner, I don't care if they read reversed cards or not. I'm not a 'back seat driver' and if my intuition leads me to a particular oracle for information I need, I'm more than happy to let them obtain it in the manner that works best for them.

Falling Cards

A falling card is any card that falls from the deck when you're shuffling or handling it. It's also any card that you notice that sticks in your mind as you're shuffling the deck. Sometimes the card doesn't just fall from the deck, though. I've seen a card jump from the deck, do a slow motion double summersault, leisurely glide to the floor and coast to the querent's feet before stopping. Both the querent (who was a skeptic until then) and I stared, open-mouthed at what we'd just witnessed. Without knowing the Tarot significance of a card that falls from the deck, she laughed nervously and said, *"I guess that one really*

Falling Cards

wants me to pay attention to it."

She was right, a falling card wants you to pay attention to it because it has special meaning to the querent, the question or issue and the reading.

Most Tarot practitioners pick up the fallen card and place it face up, on the table and refer to it during the session. I take it one step further, figuring that if the card really is important, it'll go the extra mile to make its case. I pick up the fallen card, make note of it and put it back into the deck and continue to shuffle. If the card shows up in the spread, it's important to the process and the position it's in is really significant.

Once, I was in Sedona, Arizona with my dear friend, David. We'd been told by our Spirit Guides that we needed to drive to Sedona and be there on Christmas day. We did as we'd been instructed and arrived just as the Sun was setting on Christmas Eve. Later that evening, David and I sat with our Tarot decks and asked why it had been so important for us to be there. As I shuffled my cards, the Star card leapt from the deck and landed upright on the table. As was my custom, I put it back into the deck and continued to shuffle. We got a lot of answers but the Star card didn't show up again. Finally, exhausted after a long day, we bade each other good night and David returned to his room.

The next morning, Christmas, David and I got into my car to drive to a restaurant for breakfast. The car wouldn't start. Instead of being upset about it, I felt strangely calm. We went back to our respective rooms and David called a taxi company while I called AAA. The AAA dispatcher told me that he had a lot of calls before he could get to my car and suggested we call him again after breakfast.

When our taxi arrived, I laughed. It was a long limo version of my car. On the way to the restaurant, our taxi driver asked us why we'd come to Sedona. We answered, *"We don't know why we're here. Our Guides told us that it was important for us to be here on Christmas day, so we're here."*

She replied, *"Oh, you're here because you have to go back to a vortex that was very important to you on your first visit here. You let other people convince you that it wasn't important and you forgot about the powerful connection you have to it. I haven't gotten it pin-pointed on the grid yet, but I should have all of the co-ordinates by the time I pick you up after breakfast. That is, assuming you want me to pick you up after breakfast?"*

David and I spontaneously and simultaneously shouted, *"Yes!"*

As we pulled up to the restaurant, I remembered my manners and I said, *"This is David and I'm Sheilaa. What's your name?"* She turned to us and with a beaming smile on her face, answered, *"Star."*

David and I were so excited we could hardly eat breakfast. We did the best we could and were waiting in front of the restaurant when Star returned. As she drove, she told us, *"I've got all the co-ordinates and know exactly where on the grid I'm supposed to take you."*

She drove us to the vortex at Airport Mesa. Airport Mesa was the first vortex that David and I had visited on our first trip to Sedona. We'd had one of the most powerful, intense spiritual experiences of our lives during our time there (one that for me, continued to play out for weeks and involved a Yoruba investiture ceremony, a woman who actually flew and me passing an initiation-recruitment test I didn't know I was taking). We let other people who claimed to know, talk us into discounting our Airport Mesa experience because they thought more powerful experiences could be had at other vortexes.

Significators

There at Airport Mesa, she gave us a powerful meditation, *"The Library of Knowledge,"* which I later recorded, and led us to the exact spot that David and I stood on that first visit when Courthouse rock opened up and revealed its secrets to us.

Afterwards, she dropped us off at our rooms. David suggested I call AAA so that they could start the car for us. I told him, *"We don't need them. The car will start now."* He was skeptical until I got into the car and started it. I explained, *"We knew we had to be here on Christmas day. The only reason the car wouldn't start before was so that Star could take us back to Airport Mesa. That's what our Guides wanted. Now that we've done that, we can drive anywhere we want."*

Will all falling cards take you on such an exciting adventure? You never know. What you can be certain of, though, is the falling card's influence is important and can go far beyond the cards on the table.

Significators

A significator card in a Tarot spread is one that is said to represent the querent during a Tarot reading. Significator cards are usually chosen from the Court cards and are used to represent the querent's gender, age and station in life.

In olden times, when a person's world was very small and their range of options was very narrow, the use of specific significator cards in a Tarot spread was probably helpful. Since everyone in their little world had the same or similar familial origins, it was easy to assign certain, specific traits to the querent and use a particular Tarot card to represent them. These designations were determined by combinations of the Court cards and the suit cards of the Minor Arcana:

Significators

- Pages were used to represent an immature boy or girl
- Knights were used to represent a young man in his late teens to early twenties
- Queens were used to represent an adult female
- Kings were used to represent an adult male

- Wands represented a person who had pale skin, blue or green eyes and blond hair
- Cups represented a person who had pale skin, blue or green eyes and brown hair
- Swords represented a person who had medium tone skin, hazel eyes and dark hair
- Pentacles represent a person who had olive skin, brown eyes and black hair

However, time has moved on and everyone's world is a much larger place now, and much more diverse. The old designations don't work (if they ever really did).

With this system, how would a person of color choose their significator? How would an LGBT teen-age girl choose hers? How would a first generation child of immigrants who wants to break family tradition choose his?

In addition to being limited in scope, the old designations are also stagnant. They're not only stuck in a time and place, they're also stuck energetically. The definition of the word, significator, is *"that which signifies or identifies."* The purpose of the significator card is to tell us something about the querent and their issue that would help in understanding them and finding a solution to their problem.

The querent and their issue are 'alive'—constantly shifting, changing, evolving. What might have identified them in the past may not be the energy that identifies them and their issue at the time of the session. When I want to use a significator card for a querent, I have them pull one from the whole deck at the beginning of the session. The card pulled in 'real' time accurately reveals very important information about the querent and the reason they booked a reading.

Almost all of my Tarot spreads have a "heart of the matter" position and that's where I place the significator card. The heart is the engine that runs our 'body-machine' and the card that represents the "heart of the matter" and the significator of a person or an issue are one and the same to me. When the querent chooses their significator or "heart of the matter" card in 'real' time, they reveal the very essence of their issue or problem and when that happens, the solution to their problem will begin to present itself, often in the most obvious manner.

Expiration Dates

How long is the information from an Intuitive consultation valid? Each practitioner has their own inner 'calendar' which responds to and reflects their energy and the expansiveness of its range.

It's been my experience that my information is solid (holds its form) for a six month to 1-year time period. After that, the energy gets shaky and the picture begins to diffuse. Life is organic and, therefore, it's constantly changing and so are we.

Within a six month to 1-year time period, a lot can happen. The more pro-active you are, the faster you'll move events along. Once the foreseen events are in motion, there is space for newer events, people and circumstances.

Often, you can't push the river of time, but when you find that you can, take advantages of those moments and push it for all you're worth.

Recommended Reading

1 - *Tarot For Yourself Workbook* by Mary K. Greer
2 - *Mythology* by Edith Anderson or *Bullfinch's Mythology* by Bullfinch
3 - *How To Read A Person Like A Book* by Gerald Nierenberg and Henry Calero
4 - Numerology (any small volume will do)
5 - A Thesaurus (synonyms & antonyms of words)
6 – A book on colors and their meanings (any small volume will do)
7 – *The Alchemist* by Paulo Coelho
8 – Watch the film, *Red Violin*

How to Shuffle Your Deck

This question is one of the top five questions I'm asked about learning the Tarot, *"A Tarot deck is bigger than a deck of regular playing cards, how do I easily and effectively shuffle the cards in a Tarot deck?"*

The answer to that question is the same answer to this question, *"How do you get to Carnegie Hall?"*

Practice, practice, practice.

The Tarot deck is often bigger than a deck of regular cards and therefore appears to be more difficult to manipulate. But just like everything else in life, the more you work with the Tarot deck, the

How to Shuffle Your Deck

easier it becomes to handle it. Shuffle the Tarot cards the same way you shuffle a regular playing deck. Your hands will eventually get used to the larger size of the cards and you'll forget that you were ever daunted by the prospect of shuffling them.

And don't worry about trying to channel that former life as a card shark when you handle the cards. All that really matters is that you put your energy into them and randomize their order by mixing the cards up.

If you find it difficult to hold the cards and shuffle, you can very easily, effectively achieve your goal of energizing and randomizing the cards by placing them face down on a table and gently moving them around until the neat deck of cards is spread all over the table like a big, random jig-saw puzzle.

When you feel that the cards are randomized enough, gather them back together into a neat pile. The cards are now shuffled and ready to be used.

— 6 —
Liberating Terminology, Color Symbology, Numerology

The Tarot is an ancient Intuitive Art and some of its terminology reflects the attitudes and beliefs of its antiquity. Some of the terms and phrases used in describing energy seem to specifically refer to gender in such a way that, today, they'd be considered demeaning, inappropriate and/or incorrect. Phrases like:

- Positive-negative
- Masculine-feminine
- Light-dark
- Strong-weak
- Active-passive
- Final outcome

In olden times, words like positive, masculine, light, strong and active were used to describe a conscious, activating, obvious, outgoing or intellectual energy. These words were used to describe what was considered a superior use of energy in a male-dominated society with a narrow world view.

Today, we have a more expansive view of the world and have an opportunity to see things from a more balanced, neutral perspective. The Eastern symbol for balance, Yin-Yang, is a perfect visual explanation of the strength of darkness within light and lightness within the dark. Neither is stronger than the other, they work together to produce harmony.

Liberating Terminology, Color Symbology, Numerology

Many Tarot spreads have a card that represents the 'final' outcome. Final means the absolute, concluding end. I feel it's misleading in a spread because life and we are organic, everything morphs into something else—there really is no 'final' end. The word, final, lulls you into thinking that nothing more will happen. I prefer to just use the word, 'outcome' or the phrase, 'probable outcome' because they imply that there is room for the 'outcome' to do what all outcomes do in life, transform into its next stage of development.

If, in studying the Tarot, you find that certain words or phrases bother you, please feel free to take out your thesaurus and find words or phrases with the same meaning that don't offend you.

Color Symbology and the Tarot

Color itself is a powerful, evocative symbol. The first impressions you get of a card are usually the colors. Colors are made up of energy patterns that affect us consciously and subconsciously. As a visual species, we are drawn to (or repelled by) color and light. Just seeing certain colors can shift a person's mood up or down. Different cultures respond or react differently to colors and have their own meanings for each color.

In Asia, for instance, the color white (which is the inclusion of all colors) is seen as a color of mourning and in the West it's seen as a color of innocence or purity. The color red is seen as a symbol of celebration and happiness in Eastern cultures and it symbolizes sexuality, urgency and warning in Western cultures. The color black (which is the absence of all colors) is viewed in many parts of the world as the color of conservatism and formality. In the West, in addition to symbolizing formality and the fashionably chic, it also symbolizes mourning.

Liberating Terminology, Color Symbology, Numerology

The colors on a card describe or set the mood of the card and its messages. Knowing the meanings of the colors and what they represent can often be of more value to a Tarot practitioner than knowing the meaning of a particular card.

I encourage you to get a book (a small volume will do) on colors and their meanings and study one of the most important aspects of the Tarot. Here is a brief list of primary, secondary and tertiary color symbology and their Tarot associations:

The Primary Colors are: red, yellow and blue

The Secondary Colors are: produced by combining two primary colors

The Tertiary Colors are: produced by combining three primary and/or tertiary colors

RED (primary): action, courage, strength, sex, physical energy, passion, force, urgency, engines, adventure, recklessness, optimism, travel, healing, movement, the head
Element of Fire = Wands

ORANGE (secondary): *Red plus Yellow*—energy, vitality, authority, childhood, play, creativity, innocence
Element of Fire = Wands

YELLOW (primary): Mental equilibrium, intellect, belief systems, air, breathing, urgency communication, the lungs, the arms, the hands and shoulders
Element of Air = Swords

GREEN (secondary): *Blue plus Yellow*—growth, increase, emotion, desire, harmony, money, wealth, manifestation, fertility, stability, the mundane, health, order, systems
Element of Earth = Pentacles

BLUE (primary): peace, value—especially self-value, expression, memory, receptivity, creativity, calmness, healing
Element of Water = Cups

PURPLE, VIOLET, BLUE-VIOLET, INDIGO (secondary): *Blue plus Red*—intuition, 3rd eye, protection, guidance, connection to Higher and/or Spiritual Powers and Truths, ethereal, the Universe, Akashic and other Spiritual records
Element = All

WHITE: intuition, 3rd eye, protection, guidance, purity, essence, connection to Higher and/or Spiritual Powers and Truths
Element = All

BLACK: primal, the unknown, earth, foundation, the infinite, fathomless, density, power, secrets
Element = All

SILVER: feminine, emotions, dreams, intuition, family, home, Lunar energy, the Moon, spirituality, illusion, creativity, drugs, alcohol, the stomach, the breasts
Element of Water = Cups

GOLD: masculine, activating, passionate expression, Solar energy, the Sun, romance, artists, children, fun, royalty, the ego, the heart, the spine
Element of Fire = Wands

BROWN (tertiary): *Red plus Yellow plus Blue*—of an earthly or practical nature, substance, manifestation, production, physical, responsibility, money, success, profession, land, foundation, the knees, bones
Element of Earth = Pentacles

GRAY (secondary and tertiary): *Black plus White*—wisdom, union of opposites, murkiness, cloudiness, neutrality, responsibility, rebel, uniqueness, partners, balance, the kidneys
Element of Air = Swords

Numbers and the Tarot

Numbers are a language unto themselves. They act as markers on the path of life. From the very simple to the most complex numbers, they tell us who we are, where we are, what we're here to do, how much time we have, how much we have and whether we have enough.

As a marker or gauge for the Tarot, numbers help us interpret or de-code the secrets and messages of this ancient information retrieval system. Sometimes, in a reading, the number on a card is more important than the other symbols on it and will accurately guide you to the right answer.

In numerology, all numbers are reduced to single digits, each one representing a different energy and stage of progression. In the Tarot, there are four levels or stages of completion. Three of these stages are made up of three numbers and the last or final stage is made up of one number.

The numbers on a card tell us where we are and point to the importance of what's happening. Knowing the meanings of the numbers and what they represent can be just as valuable to a Tarot practitioner as knowing the meaning of a particular card.

I encourage you to get a book (a small volume will do) on numerology and study this very important aspect of the Tarot. Here is a brief list of numbers and their Tarot associations:

1 or Ace - beginnings, possibility, birth, potential, emergence, fragility, inspiration

2 - commitment, relationship, formulation, meeting, balance, negotiation, co-operation, coming together

3 – *the initial stage of completion,* communication, choices, celebration, acknowledgement, satisfaction, realization, receptivity, receiving, results

4 - organization, foundation, order, achievement, introspection, stagnation, dissatisfaction, blocks, makes some type of statement about the circumstances

5 – the mind, change, communication, responsibility, instructions, perceptions, perspective, clarity, decisions, self-deception, the "how to" card or number

6 – *the second stage of completion,* assessment, relationship, balance, art, refinement, music, victory, peace, entrepreneurial success, insight, appreciation, trust, compassion, the gift

7 - *the most personal number,* your own inner truth, faith, inner conviction, personal decisiveness, the mystic or seeker, the spiritual path, spirituality, mystery, intuition, silent or inner wisdom, aloneness, listening, inner stillness

Liberating Terminology, Color Symbology, Numerology

❧ **8 - *the most spiritual and infinite number*** (when this number is turned sideways, it forms the lemniscate, the symbol for infinity), spirituality in form, success, money, property, business, government, immortality, security, stability, contracts, taxes, time, maturity, work, the body, the status quo, resistance, profit,

❧ **9 – *the third stage of completion,*** culmination, validation, justification, intuition, a form of success

❧ **10 – *the final stage of completion,*** conclusion, contentment, reward, success, the best, the most, fullness, fulfillment, profit, maturity of a person or thing, communion with self and the world, the end of one phase and the beginning of another

A Professional Intuitive's Perspective on The Fool

"It is only by risking ourselves from one hour to another that we live at all."
William James

Traditionally, The Fool card in the Tarot deck is often dismissed as an indicator of rashness, ridiculousness, immaturity and/or lack of discipline.

Fortunately, I am not a traditionalist. Therefore, I am not bound to this very stagnant view of one of the most important Tarot cards and stages of life we are privileged to experience.

The Fool is my favorite card of the Tarot. Whenever I choose it (or more correctly, whenever it chooses me), I know the old form of my life has outlived its usefulness and I am about to change in some exciting, unexpected, profound way.

When The Fool steps into my life, I willingly become the adventurer. I become one who seeks for the sake of seeking, spurred on by a divinely mysterious impulse that compels me to discover more about myself, life and my place in it.

The Fool demands that I become the ultimate risk taker, leaving the comfort, security and familiarity of my 'nest' and stepping out on faith into the unknown with only one guarantee of safety—my intuitive certainty that since I am divinely inspired, I am also divinely protected.

A Professional Intuitive's Perspective on the Fool

The Fool invites me to step out on faith, to risk, to trust, to live, and no matter what my head 'thinks', my heart is always thrilled and I accept the invitation.

❦

I wrote this short article on The Fool for a Jester's magazine a few years ago when I was madly in love with the great adventures he takes me on. Still madly in love with life and the journeys he takes me on, The Fool continues to be my favorite card and one of the best travel buddies, ever.

My advice to you, when he calls, don't hesitate. Willingly follow him as he leads you on a customized, just for you, enriching, life-enhancing soul passage guaranteed to change your life for the better.

7

The Major Arcana

Key Words and Phrases
(with Astrological, Elemental and Chakra Correspondences)

"Life is an unfolding story in which a person's fate is determined by the development and unfoldment of their character."
Dr. Glenn Perry

This chapter is designed to stimulate and engage all of your intuitive senses. THE FOOL leads us to and through each stage of the development of the Major Arcana—we experience the journey of life through his eyes.

Each card is highlighted with a quote that describes the energy and intent of the card. The description of THE FOOL's interaction with the energy of the card further involves us in his psyche as he travels the path to awareness.

The third part of the experience gives us the astrological, elemental and chakra correspondences for each card. This is followed by a series of descriptive key words and phrases that will help you access the infinite source of information contained in the cards.

As you read these key words and phrases, you're 'priming the pump', activating your intuitive well, which will encourage the flow of information that will help you remember and interpret the energy of each card. I've left space at the end of each series of key words and phrases so that you can add to the descriptions as you discover new ways of perceiving and interpreting the energy of each card.

The Major Arcana

The Tarot, like Astrology, is an experiential Intuitive Art, and by our life experiences, we learn more about it and ourselves. As we learn more, we have the potential of expanding our 'vision', enabling us to see, feel and hear more clearly, the infinite source of information available to all of us.

As an Astrologer and Tarot Master, it's been my experience that several of the Major Arcana cards have additional or different astrological, elemental and chakra correspondences than the traditional associations that you'll find elsewhere. I've included a note about this additional or new information in the key words and phrases sections of those card descriptions, along with my reasons for the additions and/or changes.

&

"Arcana" is Latin for secrets. The Tarot deck consists of 78 cards divided into two main groups—the Major Arcana, meaning large or big secrets, which consists of 22 cards and the Minor Arcana, meaning small or personal secrets, consisting of 56 cards.

Each of the 78 Tarot cards in the deck reflects a pattern that is universal in all peoples in all cultures at all periods of history. Therefore, each card brings to your conscious mind a personal image that you relate to and can relate to the question or issue you are consulting the cards about. **The Tarot acts as a mirror to the subconscious and reveals and reflects hidden knowledge related to the querent, question, issue or energy of the moment.**

&

The Major Arcana

VERY IMPORTANT NOTE:

GENDER:

The terms "Masculine" and "Feminine" do not refer to gender. They refer, instead, to types of energy, and/or action and/or how an action takes place. The Feminine aspect is the Creative, the Generator, it feels, creates and wants. The Masculine aspect is the Activator, the Procurer, it thinks, plans and gets. Having a need or desire is Feminine; satisfying that need or desire is Masculine. They sometimes (though not always) represent actual people.

༄

Major Arcana ~ 22 Cards ~ Large or Big Secrets:

The 22 cards of the Major Arcana represent the stages of life or the processes we all go through in our lives. The Major Arcana is divided into four main groups denoting four areas of life experience, Group 1 - Impetus; Group 2 - Body; Group 3 – Mind; Group 4 - Spirit. As we experience each of these areas and stages, we are given an opportunity to live and grow. The Major Arcana represents the psychological overview, the perspective of God or the gods, a higher authority and/or something outside our immediate control.

***REMEMBER:** I've left space at the end of each series of key words and phrases so that you can add to the descriptions as you discover new ways of perceiving and interpreting the energy of each card.

The Major Arcana

All Journeys and New Beginnings Start With—

"Sometimes the only transportation available is a leap of faith."
Margaret Shepard

GROUP 1- THE FOOL - The story of the Major Arcana is the journey of **THE FOOL** as he leaves the relative safety of all he knows as he ventures out into life, growing and maturing with each new experience symbolized by the rest of the Major Arcana characters. Because we are also **THE FOOL** symbolically, his journey is our journey through any new undertaking as well as through life's sojourn. He hears and sees what we cannot—the voice of the Divine and a vision of what can be. Though his actions may appear reckless, he feels compelled to follow the instructions of the *"Front Office"*, Divine Energy, and step out on the thin air of faith, knowing that when he does so, the ground is miraculously extended and his feet land on solid ground. As he follows the Divine instructions, he intuitively knows that he has a unique energetic and spiritual soul mate connection to several seekers he has yet to meet on his journey, THE HERMIT and all of the KNIGHTS of the Minor Arcana, in the quest to live his own personal legend.

THE FOOL is one of the Tarot's chief harbingers of dynamic, irreversible change. When he appears, something new, unknown, unexpected and/or unpredictable is coming. Whether you use willingness or willfulness in dealing with **THE FOOL**, the change cannot be avoided. **THE FOOL** *card has no number and is sometimes referred to as "Key 0".*

THE FOOL – (zodiac sign - Aquarius, planet - Uranus, element – Air, part of body – ankles, Masculine) [**7th chakra – crown – purple/white**] risk, necessary risk, sudden endings and beginnings, change, unexpected occurrences, divorce, separations, mysterious impulse, divine "listening" to the "inner voice", trust in the Divine and/or the Universe, natural impulse toward change and opening life's horizons, willingness to "jump out" into that which is unknown, innocence, carefree, spontaneity, spontaneous action, uniqueness, optimism, weirdness, erratic or irrational behavior, foolishness, frivolity, travel, shock, surprise, friends, genius, insanity, inventors, inventions, astrology, science, metaphysics, freedom, revolution, electronics, computers, the Internet

The Major Arcana

GROUP 2 – BODY The first seven cards of the Major Arcana relate to Power and the Source of Power in the form of Consciousness, the Outer Concerns of Life in Society, and One's Powers and the Strength of Those Powers. The middle three cards of this first group of seven cards are called the Triad of Nature **(THE EMPRESS)**, Society **(THE EMPEROR)** and Education **(THE HIEROPHANT)**.

> *"The true Magician creates intentional change in the world through the focused use of his will."*
> Sheilaa Hite

1 - THE MAGICIAN – When **THE FOOL** meets **THE MAGICIAN**, he comes into contact with the infinite realms of possibility. When questioned by him, "What are the only two things a Magician can do?" **THE FOOL** intuitively responds, "Anything and Everything." He learns that **THE MAGICIAN**'s capricious energy is like a double edged sword, it's powerful, but must be handled carefully. **THE MAGICIAN** brings new energy, opportunities and insight. Truth and illusion are relative to him and he has the ability to talk his way into and out of any circumstance.

THE MAGICIAN – (zodiac sign – Gemini, planet – Mercury, element – Air, part of body – hands, arms, shoulders, lungs, Masculine) [3rd chakra – yellow])

ALSO

many of **THE MAGICIAN**'s attributes stem from this connection: (zodiac sign – Scorpio, planet – Pluto, element – Water, part of body – sex organs, colon, Feminine [1st chakra – base - red]) power source, activator, magic, shaman, seer, an adept in the Intuitive, Metaphysical and/or Healing Arts, healer, good health, focus, creation,

The Major Arcana

willfulness, the will, willingness, will power, skill, control, controlling, consciousness, gambler, trickster, manipulator, lying, liars, con artist, merchant, foresight, inner guidance, dreams, catalyst, intuition, strange "twists of fate", motivation, legacies, mystery, insurance, sex, transformation, surgery, surgeons, police, military, psychology, blockage, intensity, cycle of life and death, power, focus, transformation, compulsion, decay, atomic energy, criminal, desire, extremes, anger, rage, tyranny, vindictiveness, vengeance, revenge

The Major Arcana

> *"Spirit requires a balance of female and male energy,*
> *Yin and yang, receptiveness and expression.*
> *Seek to find a balance in being and doing in all areas of your life."*
> Joyce Irvine

2 - THE HIGH PRIESTESS - When **THE FOOL** encounters **THE HIGH PRIESTESS**, he becomes aware of the depth and limitlessness of his subconscious. He learns that he must consciously relate to and communicate with the spiritual and intuitive aspects of himself in order to be spiritually informed and resourced by both the conscious and unconscious realms.

THE HIGH PRIESTESS – (zodiac sign – Cancer, planet – Moon, element – Water, part of body – chest, breast, stomach, Feminine [2nd chakra – orange]

ALSO

many of **THE HIGH PRIESTESS'** attributes stem from this connection: zodiac sign – Scorpio, planet – Pluto, element – Water, part of body – sex organs, colon, Feminine) [1st chakra – base - red] source of power, generator, intuition, shaman, seer, an adept in the Intuitive, Metaphysical and/or Healing Arts, healer, secrets, passion, intimacy, intensity, deep inner knowledge, dreams, hidden passions, hidden patterns, motivation, seduction, sensuality, sexuality, fascination, seeds of change, an individual's secret destiny, self-reliance, seclusion, receptivity, weighing the "pros and cons", choosing intuitively, the truth, women, groundedness

The Major Arcana

> *"Life is the greatest art of all,
> and the master artist is the person who is living the beautiful life!"*
> J. Edgar Park

3 - THE EMPRESS - When THE FOOL meets **THE EMPRESS**, he begins learning the earthly lessons of the continuity of life and what is required to nurture, protect and promote it for himself and for others. As he learns these lessons, his awareness extends to receiving the reciprocal benefits of honoring and respecting all life.

THE EMPRESS - (zodiac sign – Taurus, planet – Venus, element – Earth, part of body – throat, Feminine) [5th chakra – throat - blue] abundance, pregnancy, fertility, mother, Divine or Higher Power, the essence of feminine energy and creativity, maternal instinct, nurturing, creation, birth, earthiness, prosperity, inheritance, legacy, banks, gold, money, wealth, status, royalty, natural beauty, beauty products, charm, art, jewelry, nature, self-value, self-worth, self-esteem, healer, good health, sympathetic understanding, cycles of life, growth, stable relationships, love, marriage, cattle, refinement, luxury, physical beauty, singers, singing, antiquity

***When the querent asks a 'yes' or 'no' question and the Empress card comes up, the majority of the time, the answer is 'yes' because the Empress is pregnant and she'll have to deliver!

The Major Arcana

"Leaders are visionaries with a poorly developed sense of fear and no concept of the odds against them."
Robert Jarvik

4 - THE EMPEROR - As THE FOOL encounters **THE EMPEROR**, he experiences the realities of living in the tangible world of authority, discipline and conditional acceptance. Here he faces the challenges of living in society and ethically contributing to it as he seeks to establish himself by carving out his own niche.

THE EMPEROR - (zodiac sign – Aries, planet – Mars, element – Fire, part of body – head, Masculine) [1st chakra – base - red] authority, society, government, father, Divine or Higher Power, the essence of masculine energy, creativity and activity, forceful energy, dynamic energy, ambition, success, boss, law maker, rigidity, judge, domineering, arrogance, ambition, worldly power, majesty, royalty, executives, administrators, material wealth, high status, rational understanding, stability, worldly achievement, paternal instinct, males, warrior, explorer, adventurer

The Major Arcana

*"We are not human beings having a spiritual experience,
we are spiritual beings having a human experience."*
Teilhard de Chardin

5 - THE HIEROPHANT - Here **THE FOOL** meets **THE HIEROPHANT**, the messenger of the Divine, and learns that he must find the aspect of the seeker within himself. Though he is living on the earth plane, THE FOOL must seek his own connection to the "Front Office," the Divine, by developing compassion and empathy for all beings, including himself.

THE HIEROPHANT - (zodiac sign – Sagittarius, planet – Jupiter, element – Fire, part of body – hips & thighs, Masculine) [7th chakra – crown – purple/white]

ALSO

many of THE HIEROPHANT's attributes stem from this connection: (zodiac sign – Taurus, planet – Venus, element – Earth, part of body – throat, Feminine) [5th chakra – throat - blue] spiritual matters, Higher Guidance, Higher Teachings, the "big production", teacher, mentor, advisor, counselor, intuition, shaman, seer, an adept in the Intuitive, Metaphysical and/or Healing Arts, healer, healing, philosophy, spiritual mastery, moral laws, spiritual matters and discipline, blessings, protection, luck, higher education, centers of higher learning, legal papers, proclamations, declarations, high courts, churches, cathedrals, sacred spaces, travel, foreign people, countries and matters, dreams, direct experience with the Divine, long distance, foreign travel, foreigners, horses, optimism, inspiration, religion, dreams, film, cinema

The Major Arcana

"Choice is destiny's soul mate."
Sarah Ban Breathnach

6 - THE LOVERS - It's time for **THE FOOL** to meet the energy and responsibility of **THE LOVERS**. He is challenged to learn the necessity of making conscious, mature, responsible choices based on what is best instead of what stirs his emotions or desires.

THE LOVERS - although **THE LOVERS** card often shows up when a person asks about a relationship, it's not necessarily an indication of love or romance. More often, it's an indication that the querent needs to make conscious, mature, responsible choices—the very thing that's often missing whenever one is involved in a relationship!

THE LOVERS - (**zodiac sign** – Gemini, **planet** – Mercury, **element** – Air, **part of body** – hands, arms, shoulders, lungs, Masculine) [**3rd chakra** – **yellow**] responsibility, responsible mature choice, the responsibility of choosing, clear unemotional choice, consequences of choice, co-operative interaction, duality, synthesis, personal values, a need for unity, combined energies, compatibility, incompatibility, thinking, learning, planning

The Major Arcana

*"A man with outward courage dares to die,
one with inward courage dares to live."*
Lao-tzu

7 - THE CHARIOT - **THE FOOL** meets the need to learn from the inner courage of **THE CHARIOT**. He can either consciously direct the course of the energy that's roiling within him, thus shedding healing light on it as he learns to control it, or he can allow it to go unchecked and tear himself apart. The choice he makes determines the quality of his life experiences.

THE CHARIOT - (zodiac sign – Cancer, planet – Moon, element – Water, part of body – chest, breast, stomach, Feminine) [2nd chakra – orange] personal courage, harnessing the will, directing the will, focus, driving force, control, emotional courage, cars, modes of transportation, dealing with emotions (especially fear) directly and courageously, natural aggressiveness, natural competitiveness, conquest, victory, arrogance, conflict, struggle, a sense of direction, a journey of personal development, forced co-operation, travel, the military, gathering energy for a specific purpose, intuition

The Major Arcana

GROUP 3 - MIND - The second seven cards of the Major Arcana relate to the Subconscious, the Search Inward to Find Out Who We Really Are and the Laws and Agencies of the Universe. The middle three cards of this second group of seven cards are called the Triad of Change **(WHEEL OF FORTUNE)**, Outer Vision **(JUSTICE)**, and Inner Experience **(THE HANGED MAN)**.

> *"To be yourself in a world that is constantly trying to make you something else is the greatest accomplishment."*
> Ralph Waldo Emerson

8 – STRENGTH – THE FOOL encounters **STRENGTH**, who teaches him to make peace with the different aspects of himself, the primal, the ethereal, the intellectual and the emotional, by aligning himself with the strength, courage and tenderness of his heart.

STRENGTH - (zodiac sign – Leo, planet – Sun, element – Fire, part of body – heart & spine, Masculine) [4th chakra – heart – green] pride, ego issues, fear or distrust of emotions, creative blocks, self-discipline, courage, inner battles, struggle, hidden opposition, power struggles, stubbornness, issues of integrity, perseverance, determination, bigotry, hatred, drama, heart of the matter, lions, big cats, domestic cats

"To thine own self be true."
William Shakespeare

9 - THE HERMIT - THE FOOL meets **THE HERMIT** and recognizes his own need to leave the cacophonic dissonance of society behind him and seek his own personal truth. As he follows the instructions of the Divine, he recognizes his connection to his energetic and spiritual soul mates, THE FOOL and all of the KNIGHTS of the Minor Arcana, in his quest to realize his own personal legend.

THE HERMIT - (zodiac sign – Virgo, planet – Mercury, element – Earth, part of body – hands, arms, shoulders, lungs, digestive tract, Feminine) [3rd chakra – yellow]

ALSO

many of THE HERMIT's attributes stem from this connection: (10th House, sign – Capricorn, planet – Saturn, element – Earth, part of body – knees, bones, teeth, skin, Feminine) [2nd chakra – orange]

AND

many of THE HERMIT's attributes stem from this connection: (12th House, sign – Pisces, planet – Neptune, element – Water, part of body – feet, Feminine) [7th chakra – crown – purple/white] one's personal truth and the search for it, inner conviction, aloneness, introspection, wisdom, maturity, timing, discretion, patience, self-protection, the need to keep one's secrets or information to one's self, the seeker, a vision quest, teacher, guide, counselor, shaman, seer, an adept in the Intuitive, Metaphysical and/or Healing Arts, analytical, critical, maps, healing, health issues, health care, meditation, epiphany, hidden meanings, structure, responsibility, discipline, maturity, self-actualization, practical, foresight, mystery, observation, memory, experience, messenger, visions, record keeping, spiritual retreats, inspiration, deep inner knowledge, following one's destiny, self-reliance, choosing intuitively, being grounded, stealth, mundane, job, work, employees, tenants, changeable

WHEEL of FORTUNE.

The Major Arcana

"Let life happen to you. Believe me—life is in the right, always."
Rainer Maria Rilke

10 - WHEEL OF FORTUNE - THE FOOL finds himself on the **WHEEL OF FORTUNE** and comes to the realization that in the midst of stability there is always change and in the midst of change there is always stability. He recognizes that even though he cannot control the wheel, he can control the way he deals with being on the wheel, thus influencing the outcome.

WHEEL OF FORTUNE - (zodiac sign – Sagittarius, planet – Jupiter, element – Fire, part of body – hips, Masculine) [7th chakra – crown – purple/white] luck, blessings, sudden changes in fortune, higher education, travel, new phases of life, legal matters, sudden changes in status, cycles and turning points, fate, a higher authority, gambling, travel, foreign people, countries and matters, dreams, direct experience with the Divine, long distance, foreign travel, foreigners, horses, optimism, inspiration, religion, film, cinema, the "big production," the "big picture"

> *"If you understand—things are just as they are;*
> *if you do not understand—things are just as they are."*
> Zen proverb

11 – JUSTICE - THE FOOL learns impartiality from his meeting with **JUSTICE**, the balance of mind and heart in making decisions and evaluating information. He also discovers that impartiality can be a double-edged sword, too much or too little of it can be harmful, so he must learn to carefully weigh his options.

JUSTICE - (zodiac sign – Libra, planet – Venus, element – Air, part of body – liver, kidney, body's filtering system, Masculine) [3rd chakra – blue] balance, partnership, marriage, ideals, idealism, truth—inappropriate and appropriate, legal matters, contracts, the court system, attorneys, judges, diplomacy, negotiation, negotiators, mediation, mediators, justice, impartiality, ambivalence, balanced mind, fairness, objectivity, decisiveness, decision making, hostility, beauty, music, art, compromise, treaties, agreements, peace

The Major Arcana

**"It began in mystery, and it will end in mystery,
but what a savage and beautiful country lies in between."**
Diane Ackerman

12 - THE HANGED MAN - Here **THE FOOL** meets the energy of "Divine Delay" as he interacts with **THE HANGED MAN**. He learns to voluntarily surrender his impatience, fear and willfulness to the energies of that which he cannot control and find his sense of peacefulness in the gifts of trust and faith.

THE HANGED MAN - (zodiac sign – Pisces, planet – Neptune, element – Water, part of body – feet, Feminine) [7th chakra – crown – purple/white] surrender—"it's in the hands of GOD", letting go, relinquishing control in order to gain something of greater value, faith, submission, "Divine delay", being blocked or limited, patience, meditation, unavoidable delay, epiphany, a need to look at an issue from a different perspective, hidden matters, confining places, martyrs, sacrifice, unconditional love, acceptance, compassion, inspiration, devotion

The Major Arcana

"Only a creature that can think symbolically about life can conceive of its own death. Our knowledge of death is part of our knowledge of life."
Susanne K. Langer

13 - DEATH - THE FOOL dances with **DEATH** and experiences the mortality and resurrection of his ego, a beautifully powerful, life affirming, transformational feat that insures the life and immortality of his soul.

*** **This card is NOT a symbol of physical death!**

DEATH – (zodiac sign – Scorpio, planet – Pluto, element – Water, part of body – sex organs, colon, Feminine) [1st chakra – base - red] transformation, permanent end of something, death, re-birth, irrevocable change, inevitable changing cycles of the endings and beginnings in life, surrender— "it's in the hands of God", the need to let go, sexuality, control issues, bigotry, hatred, investments, other peoples resources, inheritance, corporations and governments resources, police, power, surgery, healing, politics and politicians, resurrection, investigation, in-depth research, the voice of conscience, repentance, transformation, willfulness, the will, willingness, will power, healer, healing, politics, investments, corporations and government resources, inheritance, magic, power, focus, compulsion, decay, atomic energy, criminal, desire, extremes, anger, rage, tyranny, vindictiveness, vengeance, revenge

"Can it then be that what we call the 'self' is fluid and elastic? It evolves, strikes a different balance with every new breath."
Wayne Muller

14 – TEMPERANCE - THE FOOL meets the embodiment of his higher self when he encounters **TEMPERANCE**. Through her, he learns that life achieves its own alchemical harmony if we maintain balance by mindfully pouring from the cup of the heart into the cup of the mind and back again as we firmly stand with one foot on solid ground and the other in the waters of Spirit.

TEMPERANCE - (zodiac sign – Sagittarius, planet – Jupiter, element – Fire, part of body – hips, Masculine) [7th chakra – crown – purple/white] balance in action, harmony, alchemy, co-operation, compatibility, relationship, marriage, partnership, negotiation, mediation, living in the moment, contentment, assessment, flow, balanced heart, natural justice, prosperity, abundance, success, winning, peace, Divine assistance, appropriate truth, messenger, compassion, healing, good health, the unrestricted flow of feelings, taking responsibility for one's own sense of balance and well-being, "fluid" balance, mature harmonious expression, luck, higher education, travel, new phases of life, legal matters, a higher authority, gambling, travel, foreign people, countries and matters, dreams, direct experience with the Divine, long distances, foreign travel, horses, optimism, inspiration, religion, film, cinema, the "big production"

The Major Arcana

GROUP 4 - SPIRIT - The last seven cards of the Major Arcana relate to the Super-conscious, the Development of Enlightenment and Spiritual Awareness and the Causes and Effects of Our Development. The middle three cards of this last group of seven cards are called the Triad of Inner Revelation (**THE STAR**), Mysteries of the Soul (**THE MOON**) and the Consciousness of the Life Force (**THE SUN**).

"Fear is completely dependent upon a narrow and limited sense of self. Freedom from fear lies in the awareness of it."
The Daily Guru

15 – THE DEVIL – As **THE FOOL** communes with **THE DEVIL**, he learns to free himself from his fears by acknowledging and accepting all of himself, the ugly parts as well as the pretty parts. As he does so, he releases the shame and self-imposed limitations brought about by repressing his true nature.

THE DEVIL - (zodiac sign – Capricorn, planet – Saturn, element – Earth, part of body – knees, bones, teeth, skin, Feminine) [2nd chakra – orange] control and power issues or struggles, money, attachment, secret relationships, hidden passions, sexuality, instinct, fear and fascination, doubt, pessimism, stagnation, bigotry, hatred, shame, raw and natural energy, emotional trade-offs—"Is the screwing you're getting, worth the screwing you're getting?", choosing to ignore the truth, bureaucracy, business, structure, partnership, politics, the "old boy network", the government, authority issues, social law, fame or infamy, conservative, restrictions, responsibility, material success or failure, discipline, time, old age, practical, cautious, maturity, stagnation, crystallization, stinginess, karma, *that which we consciously and unconsciously loathe, fear and despise about ourselves that is at the same time a natural part of us,* the projection of all this onto others

The Major Arcana

*"In every crisis there is a message.
Crisis is nature's way of forcing change—breaking down old structures,
shaking loose negative habits so that something new
and better can take their place."*
Susan L. Taylor

16 - THE TOWER - Here THE FOOL enters and climbs to the top of **THE TOWER** and for the first time, sees it for what it is, a symbol of outmoded values, relationships and circumstances. He realizes that it no longer reflects or supports his truth and it must come down.

***Contrary to traditional beliefs, THE TOWER is not ruled by Mars. In every way it exhibits and exemplifies the energy of the planet that destroys old outmoded forms, Uranus. At the time the Tarot came into being, Uranus hadn't been discovered yet. Mars was the only planet that had an energy remotely close to the actions and energy of THE TOWER then, so it was (temporarily) assigned the ruler of this card.

THE TOWER - (zodiac sign – Aquarius, planet – Uranus, element – Air, part of body – ankles, Masculine) [**7th chakra – crown – purple/white**] disruption, separation, divorce, unexpected and unpredictable changes or occurrences, the collapse of old forms, facades and outgrown values, a necessary and life transforming spiritual awakening and/or realization, electronics, computers, the Internet, uniqueness, rebels, large groups and associations

The Major Arcana

*"Become a possibilitarian.
No matter how dark things seem to be or actually are, raise your sights
and see possibilities—always see them, for they're always there."*
Dr. Norman Vincent Peale

17 - THE STAR - THE FOOL experiences the Divine gift of Hope as he travels with **THE STAR**. She offers him the uplifting promise of better things to come as he surveys the wreckage of the past and prepares to move beyond it.

THE STAR - (zodiac sign – Aquarius, planet – Uranus, element – Air, part of body – ankles, Masculine) [7th chakra – crown – purple/white] hope, deep inner faith, inspiration, inner awareness, active imagination, higher communications, electronics, computers, the Internet, telephones, friendship, the unexpected, spontaneity, uniqueness, the Intuitive and Metaphysical Arts, inventions, astrology, freedom

The Major Arcana

"When two people dream the same dream, it ceases to be an illusion."
Philip K. Dick

18 - THE MOON - THE FOOL, at last secure within himself, sees the beauty of his soul reflected in the light of THE MOON. As THE MOON's light bathes him in its glow, he aligns his own self-nurturing energy with hers and intuitively knows he will always find a safe haven with her.

***THE MOON card energy has often been described in traditional texts as a sign of deception, lack of clarity, confusion, illusion and/or unrealistic ideas. While there are other interpretations, these are the ones that seem to be used the most, which is unfortunate because THE MOON is so much more than that. THE MOON rules women and is the planet of intuition. Tarot is an Intuitive Art, i.e., a feminine art. These traditional descriptions and texts were written at a time when inner or intuitive activity was considered an inferior use of energy in a male-dominated society with a narrow world view.

THE MOON - (zodiac sign – Pisces, planet – Neptune, element – Water, part of body – feet, Feminine) [7th chakra – crown – **purple/white**] intuition, shaman, seer, an adept in the Intuitive, Metaphysical and/or Healing Arts, foresight, fluctuation, mystery, observation, memory, understanding the unconscious, inner self, introspection, elusiveness, illusion, delusion, confusion, deception, self-deception, uncertainty, lying, irrational fear, depressions, emotions, home, family, mother, the soul, the public, publicity, advertising, messenger, dreams, vague feelings, visions, meditation, paranoia, instability, the past, karma, childhood, oceans, water, liquids, impressionable, martyrs, unconditional love, change, sponges, record keeping, faith, receptivity, spiritual quests and retreats, compassion, devotion, inspiration

The Major Arcana

> *"This is the purpose of life, to get what you want.*
> *There are deeper things, but this is fun."*
> Karl Lagerfeld

19 – THE SUN - **THE FOOL**, having learned to love himself, welcomes **THE SUN** into his heart. Owning his Light and his right to be, he creatively takes center stage and joyfully lives out the play of his life.

THE SUN — (zodiac sign – Leo, planet – Sun, element – Fire, part of body – heart & spine, Masculine) [4th chakra – heart – green] the life force, vitality, clarity, enlightenment, optimism, enthusiasm, consciousness, art, gold, wealth, success, fame, royalty, a "star", victory, prizes, freedom, harmony, ego issues, pride, vanity, braggarts, romance, children, playing, speculative investments—real estate, stocks and bonds, creativity, actors, performers, entertainment, the stage, show business, charisma, teachers, teaching, good health, drama, magnetic, lions, big cats, domestic cats

The Major Arcana

> *"You gain strength, courage and confidence by every experience in which you stop to look fear in the face. You must do the thing you think you cannot do."*
> Eleanor Roosevelt

20 – JUDGEMENT - THE FOOL courageously descends into his shadowy depths and shines the light of truth on all that is hidden there. By exposing the darkness to the light of consciousness, he transforms himself as he reclaims his power and resurrects his dreams.

JUDGEMENT - (zodiac sign – Scorpio, planet – Pluto, element – Water, part of body – sex organs, colon, Feminine) [1st chakra – base - red] assessment, responsibility, synthesis, insight, summation, the end of a chapter in life, karma, consequences, accountability, self-confrontation, uncovering hidden information, the necessity to be honest with one's self, resurrection, investigation, in-depth research, the voice of conscience, repentance, transformation, death, re-birth, healer, healing, politics, investments, corporations and government resources, inheritance, legacies, insurance, surgery, surgeons, the military, psychology, intensity, willfulness, the will, willingness, will power, magic, power, focus, compulsion, decay, atomic energy, criminal, desire, extremes, anger, rage, tyranny, vindictiveness, vengeance, revenge

The Major Arcana

"...and the end of all our exploring will be to arrive at the place and know it for the first time."
T.S. Eliot

21 - THE WORLD - THE FOOL meets himself in the image of **THE WORLD** and unconditionally recognizes and accepts his greatness as he acknowledges the accolades of an admiring public. Having reached the completion of his journey as **THE WORLD**, THE FOOL is re-inspired and prepares to set off again on a new odyssey.

THE WORLD - (zodiac sign – Capricorn, planet – Saturn, element – Earth, part of body – knees, bones, teeth, skin, Feminine) [2nd chakra – orange] achievement, acknowledgment, success, winning, triumph, successful conclusion, union, wholeness, completion, harmonious blending of opposites, power, empowerment, inner healing, wealth, status, fame, protection, honor, infinite potential, self-actualization, the government, authority issues, responsibility, power, protection, manifestation, structure, money, career, profession, fame, infamy, structure, discipline, practical, maturity, money, conservative

— 8 —

The Minor Arcana

Key Words and Phrases
(with Astrological, Elemental and Chakra Correspondences)

*"Recognize that life is what you get when you're born ...
living is what you do with it."*
Jim Allen

This chapter on the Minor Arcana is designed along the same lines as the previous chapter on the Major Arcana. It, too, is designed to stimulate and engage all of your intuitive senses. Each suit is highlighted with a quote that describes the energy and intent of the suit.

The Minor Arcana cards are also connected to astrology and the elements. The list of these correspondences is followed by a series of descriptive key words and phrases that will help you access the infinite source of information contained in the cards.

Remember, as you read these key words and phrases, you're 'priming the pump', activating your intuitive well, thus encouraging the flow of information that will help you remember and interpret the energy of the cards. I've left space at the end of each series of key words and phrases so that you can add to the descriptions as you discover new ways of perceiving and interpreting the energy of each card.

The Tarot, like Astrology, is an experiential Intuitive Art—by our life experiences, we learn more about it and ourselves. As we learn

The Minor Arcana

more, we have the potential of expanding our 'vision'—enabling us to see, feel and hear more clearly, the infinite source of information available to all of us.

As an Astrologer and Tarot Master, it's been my experience that several of the Minor Arcana cards have additional or different astrological and/or elemental correspondences than the traditional associations that you'll find elsewhere. I've included notes about this additional and/or new information in the key words and phrases sections of those card descriptions.

"*Minor Arcana*" is Latin for small or personal secrets. The 56 cards of the Minor Arcana represent life, life's experiences and our power or control in it. Representing our "hands-on" input in our experiences and how we personally deal with what we create or encounter in life, the Minor Arcana details the journey we all take in a more personal manner than the Major Arcana. As with the Major Arcana, ***the cards of the Minor Arcana also act as a mirror to the subconscious and reveal and reflect hidden knowledge related to the querent, question, issue or energy of the moment.***

VERY IMPORTANT NOTE:

GENDER:

The terms "Masculine" and "Feminine" do not refer to gender. They refer, instead, to types of energy, and/or action and/or how an action takes place. The Feminine aspect is the Creative, the Generator, it feels, creates and wants. The Masculine aspect is the

The Minor Arcana

Activator, the Procurer, it thinks, plans and gets. Having a need or desire is Feminine; satisfying that need or desire is Masculine. They sometimes (though not always) represent actual people.

❦

Minor Arcana ~ 56 Cards ~ Small or Personal Secrets:

The Minor Arcana consists of three groups:

- ❦ Suits
- ❦ Numbered Cards
- ❦ Court Cards

The Minor Arcana is also divided into four suits of 14 cards each. Each suit represents the energy of a different element and expresses a particular area of life in specific detail from the perspective of the suit:

- ❦ Wands
- ❦ Cups
- ❦ Swords
- ❦ Pentacles

***REMEMBER:** I've left space at the end of each series of key words and phrases so that you can add to the descriptions as you discover new ways of perceiving and interpreting the energy of each card.

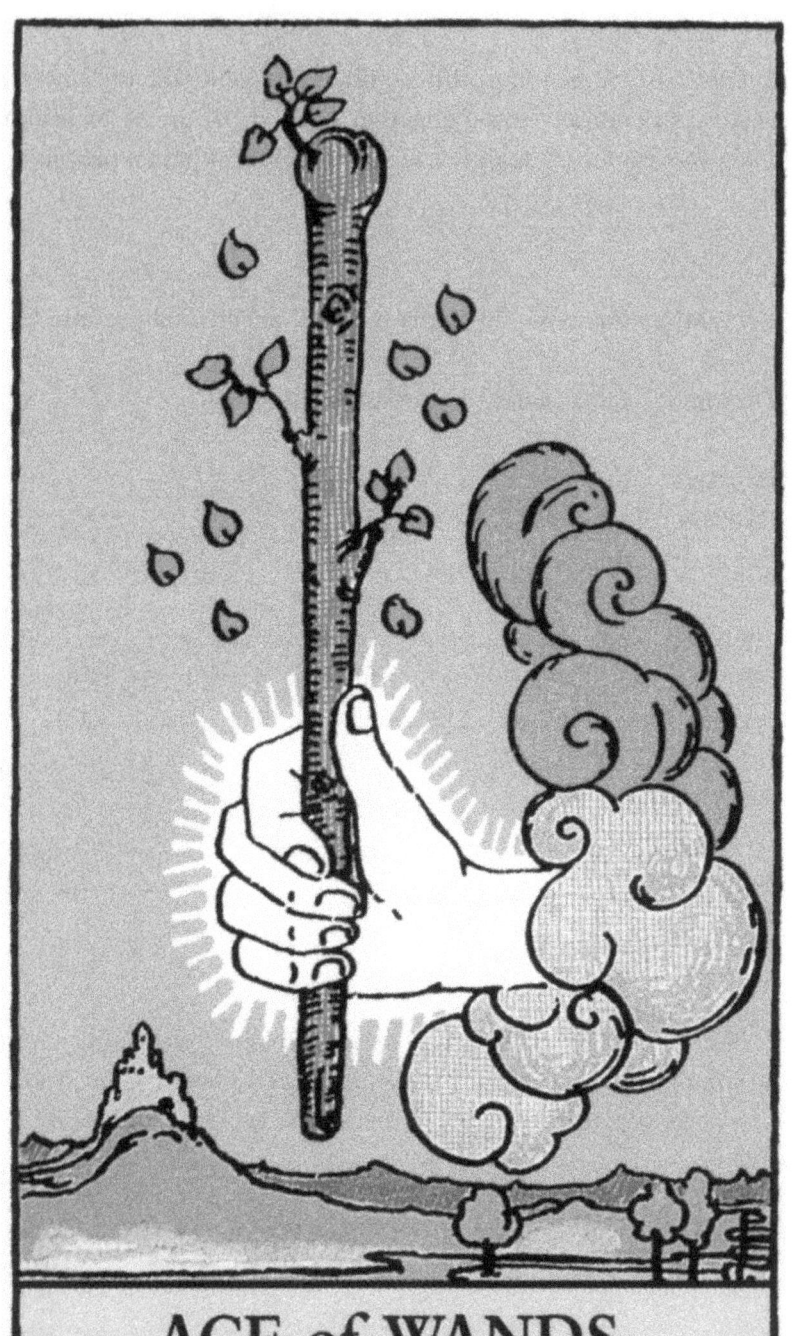

The Minor Arcana

Suits

"People are always blaming their circumstances for what they are. I don't believe in circumstances. The people who get on in this world are the people who get up and look for the circumstances they want, and if they don't find them, they make them."
George Bernard Shaw

WANDS relate to the element of **FIRE** – the realm of the **SPIRIT** – **SPRING** - *the Development of Creative Imagination* – this suit's chief aim is to provide us with the "fire of life"—inspiration. When Prometheus broke one of Zeus' cardinal rules and gave fire to the humans, he gave them something greater than flames, he gave them the priceless gift of inspiration. When you are inspired, you are one with God or the gods, you are at the center of creation. No wonder Zeus was angry! He wanted to keep that blessing exclusive to himself and the other inhabitants of Mount Olympus.

WANDS - inspiration, adventure, inner vision, perception, intuition in action, luck, blessings, advanced education, entrepreneurial pursuits, independence, philosophy, dreams, travel, spontaneity, volatile energy, connection to a Higher Power, courage, optimism, potential, ego, individuality, exploration, discovery, achievement, personal identity

*** **KNIGHTS** are associated with **FIRE - SPIRIT - WANDS**

ACE of CUPS.

The Minor Arcana

> *"If any human being is to reach full maturity,
> both the masculine and feminine sides of the personality
> must be brought up into consciousness."*
> M. Esther Harding

CUPS relate to the element of **WATER** – the realm of the **HEART** – **SUMMER** - *the Development of Feelings* - this suit nurtures and reflects our feelings as we engage in and interact with the ever present, often passionate emotional energies of relationships, creativity and spirituality. What we love and hate are often just two sides of the same mirror and here we get to see the conscious, subconscious and unconscious truths and motivations for our feelings, thoughts and actions. *"Still waters run deep"* and this suit provides a strong current for the natural flow of the intuitive senses.

CUPS - emotions, relationship, creativity, intuition, art, music, rhythm, the heart, love, passion, spirituality, elusiveness, illusion, depth, receiving, receptivity, fluidity, marriage, partnership, sharing, secretiveness, bodies of water, personal issues, inner life, connection to a Higher Power, Intuitive Arts, desires, nurturing, nesting, elation, depression, friendship

*** **QUEENS** are associated with **WATER – HEART – CUP**

The Minor Arcana

"A mind once cultivated will not lie fallow for half an hour."
Edward George Bulwer-Lytton

SWORDS relate to the element of **AIR** - the realm of the **MIND – FALL -** *the Development of the Realm of the Mind* **–** this suit is the conduit for all communicative and tangible connections. A conduit is a channel for conveying something from one point to another. Each of us is a channel of expression, conveying or communicating information in such a way that it helps us use our minds to shift our perspectives, examine our directions, choose our priorities and bridge the gaps between ourselves and others.

SWORDS - communication, thought, speech, hands, arms, learning, clarity, confusion, comprehension, concepts, abstracts, plans, systems, changeability, ambivalence, sound, books, writing, papers, separation, flexibility, conflict, negotiating, contracts, maps, roadways, arteries, duality, impartiality, emotional coldness, breath, records, printing, typing, airwaves, environment, shoulders, lungs

*** **PAGES** are associated with **AIR - MIND – SWORDS**

The Minor Arcana

*"If you have built castles in the air, your work need not be lost;
that is where they should be.
Now put foundations under them."*
George Bernard Shaw

PENTACLES relate to the element of **EARTH** - the realm of **MATTER and ABILITY** – **WINTER** - *the Development of Consciousness as Form* – this suit is the *"fourth leg of spirituality,"* manifestation is spirituality in form, it's the evidence of what you have committed the four energies to. You can be inspired to create something, be emotionally stimulated by it and make plans for it, but, unless you put the proper physical energy into it, nothing productive will happen. The unit of exchange here is value for value. Stability and solidity are the sought after attributes of this suit.

PENTACLES - manifestation, form, money, acquisition, work, structure, foundation, the law, authority, government, bureaucracy, society, civilization, land, property, business, the material world, spirituality in form, commitment, the body, what is real, self-value, reward, results, challenges, conservative, dependable, security, taxes, status quo, judges, time, maturity, stability, honor, stagnation, obstacles

*** **KINGS** are associated with **EARTH - ABILITY and MATTER - PENTACLES**

The Minor Arcana

Numbered Cards

The Ace (1)

Ace (1) – potential, possibility, new beginnings, initial inspiration, desire, idea, vision or need, emergence

ACE's (1)—ARIES ENERGY

The Minor Arcana

Ace of Wands – pure bright inspiration that's equal to the brightness of your spirit, pure insight, getting a sense of something and its value before it takes the form of thought, taking on a new role, unrefined creative force, restlessness, imagination, optimism, new directions, invention, potential, primary, first, exclusive, vigorous, vital, energy, initiative, birth, emergence

Ace of Cups – desire to make it happen, the feeling that something can be done, soul, planting seeds, fulfillment, care, sensuality, fragility, potential, creativity, play, blessings, desire, intuition, beginnings, initiation, fresh, spirituality, protection, message, sensitivity, love, union, vanity, jewelry, beauty, complexity, jealousy, joy, feminine, harmony, charm

Ace of Swords – idea, plan, ability to create a plan and put it into profitable action, mental action necessary to create the paradigm, blueprint, "getting" the concept, it's bigger than us—a lot to "wrap our minds around", contact, strife, correspondence, imagination, curiosity, intellect, processes, difficulty, adversity, force, justice, arbitration

The Minor Arcana

Ace of Pentacles – vision, sense of idea's value, desire to manifest, manifestation, the inner knowing that you can make something happen, knowing that the value is as big as your vision, ambition, determination, motivation, setting goals, achievement, business opportunities, money, property, reward, materialism, status, money, persistence, skill

The Minor Arcana

The Number 2

2 – balance, duality, communicating the initial inspiration, desire, idea, vision or need to yourself and others, commitment, a "co-" energy—co-operate, communicate, coordinate, compare, etc.

2's – TAURUS ENERGY

2 of Wands – communicating your vision, activating your desire and vision, action, experiencing the power of sharing your vision, co-operative spirit, new outlook, validation, enterprise, spirit, possibilities, decision, ideals, travel, foreign issues, restlessness, initiative, coalesce, prelude, protection, adventure, courage, support

The Minor Arcana

2 of Cups – strong deep inner feeling that an idea can work, deep self-trust, trusting others, attraction, alignment, relationship, reconciliation, meetings, partnership, balance, co-operation, harmony, happiness, joy, androgyny, eroticism, spirituality, eruption, the unconscious, love, partnership, recognition, twin flames, meetings, balance, exchange

2 of Swords – ignore, viability, angst, stalemate, choice, pretend, facts, separation, communicating, consciousness, balanced thought, denial, immobilization, conflict, opposition, extremes, anxiety, alternatives, interchange, tension, discomfort, disaster, anxiety, disagreement, dilemma, paralysis, stagnation, polarization, impasse, unaware, negotiate

2 of Pentacles – assessing value, profitability, more willingness than experience, doing what it takes to make something happen, gathering the needed tools, getting your "ducks in a row", physical affirmation, flexibility, material fluctuation, willingness, apprenticeship, control, property, manipulation, affirmation, conservation, maintenance, commitment, formulate

The Minor Arcana

The Number 3
Represents the First Stage of Completion:
results – validation, receiving, the template

3 – results, plans, communication, first physical stage of manifestation, feedback

3's – GEMINI ENERGY

3 of Wands – first results, recognition of the feasibility of the vision's success, the possibility is alive, the sense that you can create and manifest your vision, celebration, ease, gathering, Divine input, new inspirations, initial satisfaction, clarification, decision, taking stock of progress, challenge, knowledge, skill, formulas, enthusiasm, satisfaction, realization

3 of Cups – celebration, the honeymoon phase, the self-congratulatory stage, realizing what can be, marriage, joy, abundance, contentment, emotional clarity, inner awareness, illusion, emotions, heart's desire, accomplishment, fun, entertainment, delusion, rejoicing, acting, theatre, companionship, clubs, healing, "honeymoon stage", satisfaction, reception, receiving

3 of Swords – allowing others to undermine you, dissipating energy, instead of receiving—giving too much away, giving your power away, painful results, disappointment, articulation, gloom, depression, emotional turmoil, self-undoing, realization, understanding, gossip, consequences, heartbreak, self-recrimination, shame, blame, communication

3 of Pentacles – receiving material support, money, acknowledgement, offers of help, physical proof, preparation, definition, grounding, expertise, risk, flaws, limits, character, payment, reward, acquisition, dependable, challenges, security, environment, skills, competency, professionalism, career, promotion, salary raise, land, buildings, market place, acknowledgement, initiative, incentive

The Minor Arcana

The Number 4

4 –foundation, support, stability, waiting productively, contemplation

4's – CANCER ENERGY

4 of Wands – powerful support, trusting others, trusting yourself, protection, assistance, Divine help, triumph, success, harvest, eagerness, satisfaction, pause, tranquility, relaxation, opportunities, reward, optimism, benefits, reunions, influence, empathy, fruition, liberation, consolidation, exuberance, unorthodox, gathering together

4 of Cups – self-doubt, jealousies, over-reaching, a need for grounding, emotional fear, unhappiness, suspension, perception, reassessment, recuperation, withdrawal, rest, fear, solace, introversion, solitude, inner reflection, suspicion, doubt, disappointment, emotional unhappiness, betrayal, resentment, hopelessness, introspection

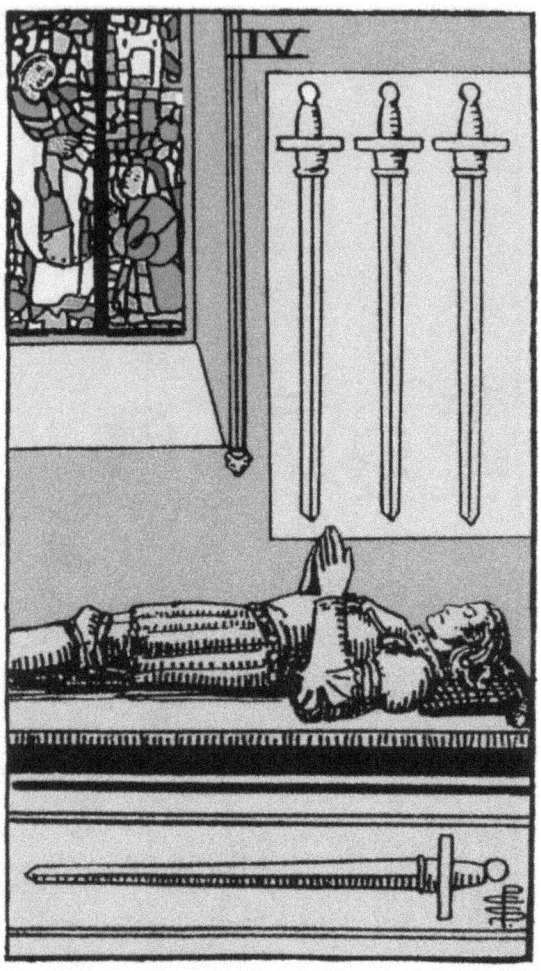

4 of Swords – waiting, contemplation, depth of commitment, ability to visualize, waiting productively—productive waiting, reality, adjustment, explanation, outline, belief systems, logic, caution, distraction, loneliness, discontentment, boredom, retreat, strength of purpose, reflection, inner peace, trust, examination, concentration, certainty, meditation, patience, doubt, statement

4 of Pentacles – foundation, physical courage, stagnation, willingness, need, necessity, practicality, pragmatism, the 'brass tacks', status-quo, non-emotional, savings, creating structure, stubbornness, inflexibility, miserliness, stinginess, lack, safety, crystallization, hardship, ice, measurable actions, productivity, "nothing ventured, nothing gained", organization, order, blocks, stagnation, intangible becomes tangible

The Minor Arcana

The Number 5

5 – the "how to" number, change, perspective, perception, the mind, choice, communication

5's – AQUARIUS ENERGY

5 of Wands – team work, intuition, grandiosity, irritations, daring, annoyance, impediments, imagination, intuitive action, courage, undaunted, , delays, adjustments, reconsidering, extremism, exaggeration, sports, competition, recklessness, destructive, independence, conflict of interest, catastrophe, apathy, integrity, argument, manipulation, responsibility

The Minor Arcana

5 of Cups – abandonment, disbelieve, grief, disillusionment, projection, channeling, emotional energy, pessimism, depression, fatigue, regret, heartbreak, bitterness, sorrow, loss, evocative, disturbance, illness, release, distress, reaction, discomfort, emotional upheaval, crisis, vulnerability, confusion, exhaustion, betrayal, rite, remorse, change, choice

5 of Swords – overwhelm, inadequacy, loss of confidence and trust, a need to change perspective, fear, focusing, unity, uncertainty, reaction, response, tension, humiliation, images, despair, distortion, understanding, struggle, androgyny, responsibility, continuity, reversal, error, influence, feedback, editing, opinions, ideas, provocation, disagreement, distortions, perceptions, responsibility, circumstances

5 of Pentacles – need to make lemonade out of lemons, practical needs, change of perspective, weakness, defeat, poverty ,experience, chaos, failure, disguise, determination, strain, extension, difficulty, survival, relief, fear, trouble, intermediary, invincibility, limitations, surrender, adaptation, resolution, instability, material values, mundane matters, tests

The Minor Arcana

The Number 6
Represents the Second Stage of Completion:
victory, assessing value, the "prototype"

6 – victory, value, rewards, creativity, money earned from your own efforts, balance, partnership, acknowledgement, encouragement

6's—TAURUS ENERGY

6 of Wands – victory, success, prototype, model, archetype, test run, powerful support, fame, award, validation, adventure, ego, certification, peak, graduation, promotion, recognition, investors, charisma, appreciation, triumph, parades, blessings, luck, fortune, satisfaction, relaxation, consistency, sense of purpose, personal identity, self-image, visions, dreams, peace, entrepreneurial success

The Minor Arcana

6 of Cups – sorting, priorities, memories, self-value, fruition, love, promises, making choices, acceptance, romance, friends, the past, recollections, hope, nostalgia, tranquility, pleasure, serenity, peace, sentiment, fantasy, cherishing, unconditional love, kindness, sharing, contentment, rhythm, lifestyle, appearance, relationship, balance, refinement, music, art, insight, compassion, Summer

The Minor Arcana

6 of Swords – trust, faith, self-trusting, fearlessness, acceptance, harmony, moving forward, approval, understanding, an open mind, willingness, agreement, emissary, interpretation, serenity, calmness, serenity, herald, consciousness, peace, insight, comprehension, cycles, affirmation, attitudes, reiteration, echo, recurrence

6 of Pentacles – money, profits, knowing your value, powerful support, investments, physical manifestation, proportions, sanctuary, truth, philanthropic, patronage, possessions, humanitarian, community, contests, gifts, donations, well-being, balance, comfort, priceless, renewal, generosity, charity, benevolence, income, assessment, appreciation

The Minor Arcana

The Number 7

7 – the spiritual path, trust, listening intuitively, competitive forces, choices, "Divine opportunity"

*** 7 is the most personal number because it's the number of your own inner truth

7's – PISCES ENERGY

7 of Wands – too much input, complications, seeking advice, consulting experts, experimentation, strength, expectation, envy, competiveness, options, alternatives, variety, expansion, excitement, exercise, attack, fights, anger, flexibility, aggression, warrior, armor, weapons, emotional fire, trial, vitality, risk, gambling, inner conviction

7 of Cups – fantasy, nightmares, daydreaming, impulse, intoxication, intuition, bewilderment, devotion, imagination, talent, diplomacy, artistry, "castles in the air", guilt, fear, evasion, charm, "too much of a good thing", prayer, worship, capriciousness, responsiveness, suffering, "rose colored glasses", stimulation, rejection, inner truth, mystic, spirituality, mystery

The Minor Arcana

7 of Swords – trust, listening to intuition, inner knowledge, insider trading, betrayal, 'walk in faith', logical use of intuition, enlightenment, secrets, gossip, lies, rumors, insincerity, deceit, second guessing, infringement, decisions, sneakiness, thievery, angst, disappointment, dissatisfaction, excuses, defensiveness, contradiction, escape, personal decisiveness

7 of Pentacles – timing, gestation, growth, self-reliance, inclusion, cultivation, ethics, wisdom, determination, hesitation, tribute, immaturity, entitlement, amorality, morals, challenge, instinct, justification, nobility, obviousness, deliberateness, stealth, requirement, bargaining, tact, desperate measures, accomplishment, premature, stillness, wisdom, aloneness

The Minor Arcana

The Number 8

8 – manifestation, status quo, belief systems, persistence, resources, commitment, time, work, success, maturity, authorities, in perpetuity, prosperity

*** the most spiritual number, when 8 is turned on its side, it becomes the lemniscate, the symbol for infinity

8's – CAPRICORN ENERGY

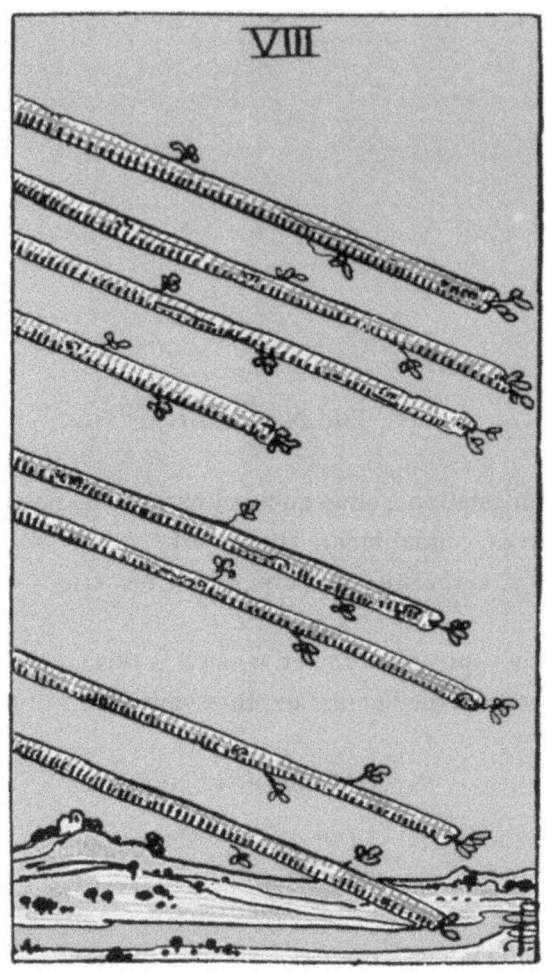

8 of Wands – the will, luck, blessings, self-confidence, strategy, "smooth sailing", laurel wreath, foreign countries, manifesting vision, synchronicity, travel, foreign languages, Supreme Court, universities, cathedrals, fast cars, emphasize, promotions, "the honeymoon card", athletes, new beginnings, change of residence, protection, stimulation, excitement

8 of Cups – need to walk away, improving your vision, vengeance, psychology, loss, exile, infinite, archaic, obsolete, museums, divorce, separation, vision quest, the unknown, emotional risk, re-evaluation, cowardice, release, emotional priorities, inner awareness, self-honesty, sacrifice, timidity, personal courage, shyness, abandonment

The Minor Arcana

8 of Swords – stuck in a mindset, results of poor planning, stagnation, shame, stubbornness, inflexible, denial, entrapment, self-sabotage, stagnation, turbulence, anxiety, distress, disturbed, humiliation, frustration, ignorance, problems, isolation, embarrassment, stifled, bondage, unconsciousness, oppression, confusion

8 of Pentacles – seriousness, rigidity, permanence, politics, conservative, cautious, established, challenge, continuity, perseverance, development, consistency, appropriateness, monotony, predictability, regulations, habits, reliability, replenishment, reserves, process, restoration, possessions, renovation, architecture, patterns, stability, security, wisdom, conformity, spirituality in form, accumulation, government, formality, immortality, taxes, time, age, work, the body, facts, mountains

Introduction

The Number 9
represents the Third Stage of Completion:
culmination, acknowledgement, fine-tuning

9 – culmination, dress rehearsal, the 'salad bowl' stage—what ingredients are in the bowl, market place value, celebration

9's – SCORPIO ENERGY

9 of Wands – rough edges need to be smoothed, exhaustion, vigilance, wariness, frustration, weariness, doubt, fear, demands, defensiveness, stamina, "darkest before the dawn", need to resource and regroup, determination, endurance, awareness, evolving, compromise, power plays, battle weary, strategy

9 of Cups – celebration, emotional satisfaction, party, "wish come true" card, contentment, fulfillment, ease, sensuality, natural flow, integration, flexibility, effortlessness, gifts, blessings, joy, excitement, achievement, exhilaration, intuition, lifestyle, mature marriage, harmony, music, art, diplomacy

9 of Swords – needless worry, unfounded fears, distrust of others, self-imposed confusion, distrust of self, "the nightmare card", unnecessary complications, need to clear your head, need a different perspective, bad influences, hypochondriac, suspicion, distrust, dysfunction, anxiety, psychosomatic illness, despair

9 of Pentacles – finite, structure, foundation, material rewards, job well done, great reputation, successful, mastery, wealthy, pride, progressive development, well-being, safety, resources, gold, public acknowledgement, expert, progress, intuition, formation, comfort, precious metals, valuable, stability, security, graduation, good health, groundedness, validation

The Minor Arcana

The Number 10
Represents the Final Stage of Completion:
fulfillment, the end and the beginning

10 – completion, end of one phase & beginning of another,
finished project, result

10's – CAPRICORN ENERGY

10 of Wands – exhaustion, self-doubt, dissatisfaction, burdens, martyrdom, oppression, responsibilities, overwhelm, stagnation, collapse, intensity, dedication, excess, inability to comprehend, dwells on negativity, impossibility, "artists overwhelm" card, plodding, self-imposed limitations, resistance, striving, poor self-image, overworked, endurance

10 of Cups – polished, completed, wonderful outcome, admired, wonder, awe, celebration, union of generating and activating selves, mature marriage, grace, gratitude, bliss, gifts, spiritual, emotional, innocence, creative aspect, joy, happiness, gold, riches, rainbows, protection, fertility, family, humanitarian, appreciation, harmony, love, art, music, perfection, the best

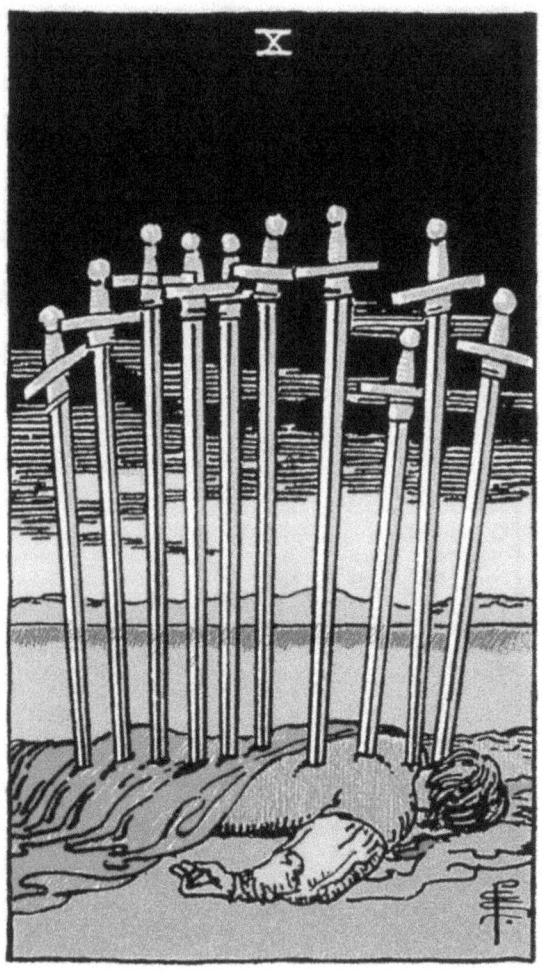

10 of Swords – exhaustion, fate, criticism, anxiety, extremism, difficult transition, over-reacting, "pity-party", destruction, pain, rebirth, hysterical, distraught, manic, weird, drama queen, conditioning, impatience, self-destruction, loss, betrayal, despair, poverty, disappointment, trials and tribulation, resolution, oppression, delusion, inevitability

10 of Pentacles – successful, completed, profitable, abundance, legacy, dynasty, in perpetuity, advantages, established, inheritance, fame, aristocracy, heirloom, birthright, gift, money, relics, power, influential, stable, wealth, privilege, hierarchy, generosity, society lineage, mastery, perfection, permanence, achievements, manifestation, worldliness, enduring, materialism, destiny, the most, maturity of a person or thing

The Minor Arcana

Court Cards

represent types of energy and character types. They DO NOT describe qualities limited to just men or women, they emphasize the active and receptive qualities of energy available to both women and men.

༃

*** VERY IMPORTANT NOTE ***
although I've stated this before,
this very important point bears repeating:

GENDER:

The terms "Masculine" and "Feminine" do not refer to gender. They refer, instead, to types of energy, and/or action and/or how an action takes place. The Feminine aspect is the Creative, the Generator, it feels and wants. The Masculine aspect is the Activator, the Procurer, it thinks and gets. Having a need or desire is Feminine; satisfying that need or desire is Masculine. They sometimes (though not always) represent actual people.

The Minor Arcana

Pages
Unfocused Energy, Unfocused Power

awareness, delicate fragile beginnings, androgynous, potential, unfocused

PAGES are associated with **AIR - MIND – SWORDS**

PAGES symbolize a new awareness, especially when that awareness is related to the self. Each of the **PAGE**'s becomes aware of his/her power, abilities or value according to the suit and element they represent. This awareness is fragile and supported only by a vague sense that they are more than they previously thought or were told. They represent the pre-pubescent stage of development in people and processes; therefore, they can be as flaky, fickle or absent-minded as any 11 to 14 year old child. **PAGE**'s also symbolize the delicate, vulnerable new beginnings of any project, process or relationship and indicate that the issue must be nurtured and handled with care. **PAGE**'s are a higher octave or level of the **ACE**'s.

The Minor Arcana

PAGE of WANDS – ARIES – awareness, enthusiasm, Spring, travel, immaturity, diminutive, danger, confidence, reckless, absent minded, running, activity, undeveloped, nascent beginnings, need for adventure, unconscious, adolescent, opportunity, risk, faith, solo, "leap before you look", revealing, optimism, lucky, protection, messenger

The Minor Arcana

PAGE of CUPS - CANCER – awareness, immaturity, innocence, sweetness, dreamy, fantasizing, day-dreaming, a romantic, new life, sensitivity, gentleness, kindness, youthful, intuitive, artistic, fragility, pre-pubescent, adolescent, opportunity, trust, nascent beginnings, embryonic, emerging, hopeful, child, self-reflection, vulnerable, changeable, self-value

The Minor Arcana

PAGE of SWORDS - GEMINI – awareness, immaturity, enthusiasm, sky, cleverness, honesty, unfeeling, calculating, gossip, incompleteness, inattention, carelessness, talk, immune, unconcerned, distrust, rumors, stars, distraction, pre-pubescent, adolescent, education, loquacious, picky, opportunity, avoidance, absent minded, thoughtlessness, weather

The Minor Arcana

PAGE of PENTACLES - TAURUS – awareness, immaturity, enthusiasm, respectful, trust funds, self-value, discovery, concentration, awe, herbs, pre-pubescent, adolescent, fertile, money, education, apprentice, seriousness, flowers, solemn, meticulousness, diligence, ambitious, appreciation, careful, nature, opportunity, promise, contemplation, hopeful

The Minor Arcana

KNIGHTS
Focused Energy, Power Beginning to Focus and Form

questing, volatile, energetic, courageous,
adventure, untamed, focus

KNIGHTS are associated with **FIRE - SPIRIT – WANDS**

❧

KNIGHTS are questers. They symbolize the energy of the idealistic seeker, always on a quest to find or experience perfection according to the suit and element they represent. Their recklessness is legendary, but without their daring, nothing new would ever be accomplished, discovered or brought into focus. Every successful venture has a **"KNIGHT"** phase, the phase where the person is either too blind, idealistic or arrogant to realize that they could fail. Thank goodness for the **KNIGHT** phase! As they follow their Divine instructions from the "Front Office," they recognize their connection to their energetic and spiritual soul mates, THE FOOL and THE HERMIT, in their quest to discover their own personal legend. They represent that thrill seeking teen-age stage, 14 to 20 years old, where life is one big adventure that's all about them.

The Minor Arcana

KNIGHT of WANDS – SAGITTARIUS – quest, focus, reckless, ego, action, daredevil, flamboyance, challenge, volatile, effervescence, movement, trendy, self-centered, careless, arrogance, changeable, hot-tempered, ambiguous, "bad boy", perspective, lucky, charisma, ingenuity, bragging, adventure, inflation, charming, unreliable, intuitive, irresponsible

KNIGHT of CUPS – PISCES – quest, focus, poetry, reckless, handsome, beautiful, soulful, lover, romantic, protection, truth, charm, charisma, mother, "knight in shining armor", ideals, perfection, fickleness, gentleness, intuitive, kindness, worship, immature, "in love", artist, musician, proposal, rescue, spiritual, untamed, imagination, youthful, senses, joy

KNIGHT of SWORDS - GEMINI – quest, focus, reckless, daredevil, speed, action, quick-witted, mercurial, thoughtful, rescue, untamed, youthful, chaos, ruthlessness, wind, weather, magnetic, self-involved, shallow, intelligence, impatience, ideas, duplicity, flexibility, turbulence, quarrelsome, change, duality, conflict, ambivalence, callousness, disruption

The Minor Arcana

KNIGHT of PENTACLES – VIRGO – quest, focus, reckless, practical, cautious, patient, rescue, untamed, youthful, stillness, "continuity of life", contemplation, perseverance, tolerance, peacefulness, trustworthy, determined, consistent, tasks, dependable, stoicism, kindness, earthy, nature, reliable, industrious, cultivation, pollination, maturity, prophecy

The Minor Arcana

QUEENS
Focused and Formed Power, the INTUITIVE USE OF LOGIC

generating, receptive, magnetic, inner power, intuition

QUEENS are associated with WATER – HEART – CUPS

QUEENS represent the creative, generating energy in life. They symbolize the source of power in the suit and element they represent. When they have a desire for something, they create and transmit the force that will attract what they need as they generate the empowering energy that magnetizes the external forces required to manifest their desires. The **QUEENS** feel, want, generate, gestate and magnetize, they are the "feelers and the wanters". Their ability to intuitively interpret logical concepts in order to glean the essence of any idea is only one of their priceless gifts.

QUEEN of WANDS – LEO – stationary, attracting, emotional expression, strength, focus, vivacious, entrepreneurial, energetic, warrior, protective, joy, enthusiasm, vibrant, courageous, intuitive, athletic, active, daring, radiance, loyalty, "productive patience", destiny, adventure, luck, protection, inner conviction, ingenuity, cleverness, faith, spirit

QUEEN of CUPS – SCORPIO – stationary, attracting, emotional nature, focus, dreamy, fashionable, romantic, intense, intuitive, diva, romance, beauty, magical, sexual, sensual, sensitivity, fascinating, healing, seductive, ethereal, fantasy, possessiveness, controlling, mystical, paradox, elusive, charismatic, love, mysterious, unknowable, alluring, joy, hypnotic, passionate

The Minor Arcana

QUEEN of SWORDS - AQUARIUS – stationary, attracting, emotional control, focus, professional, courage, misunderstood, will, determination, patience, aloofness, balance, withdrawn, intelligence, intuitive, lawyer, reflective, spiritual, idealistic, adamant, fear, independent, strength, courage, perfection, writer, integrity, nobility, isolation, cold, frustration, anxiety

QUEEN of PENTACLES - TAURUS – stationary, attracting, emotional power, focus, herbs, fertile, wealthy, successful, practical, materialistic, luxury, responsible, business, employer, intuitive, sensuality, powerful, passion, jewels, protective, the body, dignity, generosity, pragmatic, self-value, stability, endurance, pleasure, gold, resources, money, classic

The Minor Arcana

KINGS
Directed and Formed Power, the LOGICAL USE OF INTUITION

activating, dynamic, magnetized, physical power, logic

KINGS are associated with **EARTH - ABILITY and MATTER – PENTACLES**

KINGS represent the activating, dynamic energy in life. They symbolize the power source in the suit and element they represent. They are the masculine counterpart to the energy of the **QUEENS** and, as such, they translate the internal, creative forces of the **QUEENS** energy into directed, external, manifesting energy which has the ability to produce in physical form what was gestated on an inner plane. The **KINGS** think, plan, obtain and are magnetized, they are the "thinkers and the getters". Their ability to logically interpret intuitive input enables them to have access to a 360 degree view of life.

The Minor Arcana

KING of WANDS – ARIES – dynamic, activating, magnetized, explore, energetic power, strategy, direct, active, adventure, dynamic, persuasive, wit, charisma, excitement, entrepreneur, lucky, triumphant, opportunist, unreliable, salesman, dramatic, charm, brilliance, personality, leader, restlessness, impulsive, strength, nobility, wisdom, visionary, possibility, victory, fire

KING of CUPS – CANCER – dynamic, activating, magnetized, emotional power, moods, therapist, counselor, wounded healer, emotionally distant, gifted, empathy, musician, intuitive, trust, poetry, enchanting, influential, charming, boldness, teacher, compassion, paradox, ambivalence, depth, mistrust, harmony, suppression, calmness, maestro, producer, esoteric

KING of SWORDS – LIBRA – dynamic, activating, magnetized, mental power, strategy, direct, active, logic, professional, calmness, unemotional, executive, justice, fairness, lack of empathy, respect, suspicion, posture, conviction, foresight, organization, cleverness, brilliance, shrewdness, strategy, consultant, inventive, guile, determination, fairness

The Minor Arcana

KING of PENTACLES – CAPRICORN – dynamic, activating, magnetized, physical power, natural, direct, worldly power, success, perpetuity, wealth, stubborn, patient, integrity, money, executive, determination, fortification, government, wisdom, greed, ambition, status, fame, infamy, recognition, security, stability, challenges, foundation, corruption, resources, society, possessions, physical, structure

— 9 —
How to Conduct a Tarot Consultation

The most important components involved in conducting a Tarot consultation (or any other type of consultation) are Attitude, Atmosphere, Ambience.

Your Attitude, the manner in which you conduct yourself, is the single most important aspect of the three "A's". You set the tone for the consultation. As you prepare for the session and during the session, set aside any anxieties and any personal or emotional issues. This is easier than it sounds because for the length of the reading you will have someone else's issues to deal with, giving you a mini-vacation from your own.

Do whatever exercises you like that put you in a calm, comfortable mind and body frame, deep breathing, meditation, a nap, whatever works for you. Remember that the client is coming to you for advice and is most likely not very centered or grounded at this time. Your being calm, centered and grounded will help the client feel more at ease with you and give you the confidence you need as well as make it easier for your mind to align with your intuition.

The Atmosphere of the space you conduct the consultation in is important, too. You need a quiet private area, free from distractions to the eyes and ears. Both you and your client should be seated comfortably, and you will need a large enough flat, clear surface to lay the Tarot cards out on. Have a box of tissues nearby. If you decide to record your sessions, make sure the recorder and the microphone are close enough to clearly pick up your voices, but are not so close that they become obtrusive or intimidating to you or your client. Make sure the volume on your telephone answering machine is turned down and it's set to answer your phone, or un-plug the phone during the reading. It's very disruptive and disconcerting (as well as disrespectful) to your client and to the process to interrupt the session by answering the phone and/or taking calls.

As for Ambience, create a space you feel comfortable, safe, honored and welcome in. If you feel this way, your client will too. Burn incense before the client comes and during the session (if the incense burns down or goes out during the session, don't interrupt the reading to light another one). The smell of the incense creates a special feeling and helps clear your space of any negative energy. Flowers and plants—organic or inorganic, are also wonderful as part of your setting for the readings.

After your client has gone, burn Sandalwood incense in your reading space. This is very necessary because you don't want anyone else's troubles attaching themselves to you or your space. Having a crystal bowl of water in the space during the reading will also help keep your reading area clear of negative energy. At the end of the day, pour the water into the toilet and flush it.

Once a week, burn dried sage in your reading space. This will purify the area (and you) as well as help keep it balanced and clear of unwanted energy.

How to Conduct a Tarot Consultation

How to Phrase Questions During A Tarot Consultation

Knowing **HOW** to phrase a question is equally as important as the question itself if you want clear concise information that is of maximum benefit to you and your client.

Did you know that there are only three questions ever asked of anyone in an advisory capacity? No matter how it's put, those three questions are always about **love,** "When will I meet someone?" or "Are my children OK?" or "Is my pet happy?"; **money,** "Will I pass the Bar exam?" or "Is my job secure?" or "Can I afford to go on vacation?"; **health,** "Will I be fit enough to run the marathon?" "Why am I so stressed?" "Why is my Maltese, "Biddles," so overweight?"

Interestingly enough, the issue of health is a distant third. If they have love and security, most people can find the strength to deal with whatever health issues might come up for them.

Very often when a client comes to see you, they are in a state of confusion about some aspect of their lives. Sometimes they know what answers they are seeking, sometimes they don't. Since they have come to you for clarity, it is up to you to discover the pattern or source of their confusion and help them to phrase their questions correctly in order to obtain the clarity they are seeking.

The best way to do this is to spend the first few minutes of the session talking to them about why they came to see you. Even if they are not sure why they made the appointment with you, you will begin to notice certain words, phrases, and/or mannerisms that will give you very clear clues as to the cause of their confusion. These clues will often be confirmed by the intuitive feelings you get as you listen to them. As you observe and sense what is going on with your client, gently question them about these clues. Listen with all of your senses and in very little time, you will know "where it hurts" and how to go about stopping the pain, i.e., what specific questions your client needs to ask.

The more clear and specific the question, the more clear and specific the answer will be. The Universe (and everyone else) returns to us the same type of energy it receives from us. If we ask a muddled, vague question of the Universe, it will give us a muddled, vague answer.

EXAMPLES:

CLIENT: "Tell me about my love life."

YOU the
CONSULTANT: "Are you currently involved with anyone?" (You would be surprised at the number of people who ask this question who are **NOT** involved at the time!) If they are not involved, ask them if their real questions are "Will I be involved in a relationship?"; "If so—when and how will it happen?"; "If not—why and what can I do to change this?"

*   *   *

CLIENT: "What is my life's mission or purpose?"

YOU the
CONSULTANT: "Everyone's life mission or purpose is to be the most positive expression of the Creator they can be. Let's see

> how you can most beneficially contribute to your mission and have your mission beneficially contribute to you." Then, ask the client what makes them happy, what makes their heart feel good, what their dreams of happiness are. A person's life mission is always directly connected to their heart, which is where the Creator lives."

*   *   *

CLIENT: "Should I..." or "Is it best for me to..."

YOU the
CONSULTANT: "Let's look at that issue from the perspective of what is **most beneficial** for you (or 'your growth') at this time (or 'in this matter' or 'in this situation')." *** The words **'should'** and **'best'** very often carry an energy of 'other people's opinions' about what is correct for the client. The information you are looking for comes from the more neutral and accurate perspective of what is *'most beneficial'* for your client.

*   *   *

CLIENT: **1** - "What will happen in the future?" or **2** - "What will happen in my life" or **3** – "What will happen to me (or in my life) during the next week, month, year (or whatever increment of time the client is inquiring about)?"

YOU the
CONSULTANT: "We need to be more specific, **1** - At what point in the future are you asking about and in what area of your life are you concerned about? And for questions **2** or **3**, "What area of your life are you asking about?"

*** **NOTE:** *It's also a good idea to ask the client why they are asking that question. Often their motivation for asking the question is the real issue that needs to be addressed during the session.*

Timing of Events During a Tarot Consultation

"When?" "How soon?" "How long?" These are the most often asked questions during a consultation.

Determining the timing of events during a consultation is a subtle art in itself. Timing is the most difficult aspect of a consultation because time in the ethereal realm isn't calculated in the same way that time in the world of matter is calculated.

Down here on the ground, in the world of matter, we see time in a linear fashion, with each event following the other in a straight line progression. Because of this, we assume that all time and timing are calculated that way. In the ethereal realm, however, we, time and events are seen as a wheel, we or the event are the hub, the outer circle or rim is the time-line and the spokes are the energy points that connect us (the hub) to places or events on the time-line (rim).

Another very important reason that timing predictions are so elusive is this oft forgotten truth, **nothing is written in stone.** As the querent responds or reacts to their situation, they change, their energy changes and the circumstances can change. Timing is based on where the participants and the situation are at the time of the consultation. If one of the participants makes a radical change, then the energy flow that points to a particular time and event can be radically shifted, too.

How to Conduct a Tarot Consultation

As you become more experienced with the Tarot cards, you will find that you *"just know"* or *"feel"* the answers to timing questions. And you will find that at least 75-95% of the time you will be right!

Practice, patience and these guidelines will help you develop your timing skills. Remember, these are only guidelines, not hard and fast rules with any guarantee of certainty. They are only to help you develop your own subtle *"inner calendar"*.

GUIDELINES:

WANDS indicate Spring; the most fruitful period immediately following an austere or barren situation; very soon (Wands are related to fire and fire travels very quickly!); during or after the 1st phase of something; with the discovery or claiming of something; during a very hopeful, positive, risky or exciting event or time

CUPS indicate Summer; the most fruitful period or phase of something; when one is content and at peace with one's self or the situation one is in; when things are moving along in a leisurely manner (Summer is a "lazy" season); when there is agreement among all those concerned in the matter; during a very emotional event or time period

SWORDS indicate Fall; after the middle phase of something; during or after uncertain times or events; during a period of "reaping" results or benefits; during or immediately after a time of negotiations; when a contract or agreement is signed; when a legal matter is resolved; at the end of a learning phase—a graduation or certification process; when records or papers are submitted

PENTACLES indicate Winter; the end of a cycle; during a barren or austere phase; gradually; the final phase of something; when a business deal is complete; when the government or any other authority gets involved; when a person, document or object matures; when money is involved or something is finalized; when a person is in a state of acceptance; when a person or situation is grounded

The **MAJOR ARCANA**: Whenever a Major Arcana card is pulled in response to a timing question, it indicates that the matter is out of our hands and is most likely in the hands of someone or something more powerful than us.

THE FOOL indicates very soon and in a manner you least expect; indicates unexpected and/or unpredictable timing

THE EMPRESS indicates within the next few weeks or months (she is pregnant and will be giving birth soon); whatever the client is inquiring about is at least underway and moving toward completion; also indicates Spring

THE HIEROPHANT indicates timing is based on a major change and a form of Divine intervention

THE HERMIT indicates Fall; after or because of a period of seclusion, exploration or confinement

JUSTICE (the *letter* of the law) indicates dealings that involve facts and/or details; the Fall; indicate the matter is being decided on now; also September – October; after a 'harvest' time

TEMPERANCE (the *spirit* of the law) indicates a benevolent force, powerful or Divine Intervention; Spring; also November – December; toward the end of a process or time period

WHEEL OF FORTUNE indicates big changes soon; also November –

How to Conduct a Tarot Consultation

December; toward the end of a process or time period

THE HANGED MAN indicates it is definitely out of our hands and we must develop patience and faith

DEATH indicates the end of the matter and there is no recourse; it's in the process of coming to completion right now

THE TOWER indicates unexpected, unpredictable timing possibly after or because of the dismantling of an old structure or belief system

THE STAR indicates unexpected, unpredictable timing

THE SUN indicates soon unless **THE DEVIL** card is present, which will slow down the process

JUDGEMENT indicates when the truth about a situation or person comes out

THE WORLD indicates at the completion of a long process

Numbers—The numbers of the cards play a role in timing, too.

5 – indicates change; after a big change, shift or adjustment

7 – indicates that the timing is in the hands of a Higher Power and you'll have to develop faith and patience

8 – indicates maturity; in due time; as or after something nears its conclusion; timing often depends on others in positions of authority

9 or 10 – indicate that the matter is concluding and will come to full fruition soon

Sights and Sounds—

Pay attention to what comes to mind when you're determining timing. Be open and expansive in your interpretation of the information that comes to you.

Maybe you'll see or think of a clock, the numbers on it can point to the number of days, weeks or months before something comes to fruition, or weather conditions, that can often tell you the season in which something will happen, or an event which may have nothing to do with the question but gives you timing information, like the last day of school or a wedding. School ends in June for the Summer and a lot of weddings are held in June, so the answer to your timing question could be June or during the Summer.

Personality Types and Temperaments
Timing can sometimes be determined by a client's Personality Type or Temperament

Nervous or Impatient Types: Speed up the time indicated by the Suit or Major Arcana card pulled for a timing question. These types are generally operating under a faster vibration than the average Personality Type or Temperament.

Dreamy or Slow, Methodical Types: Slow down the time indicated by the Suit or Major Arcana card pulled for a timing question. These types are generally operating under a slower vibration than the average Personality Type or Temperament.

*** **REMEMBER:** Let your intuition guide you in timing issues (as well as in all other issues). If the cards indicate one direction and your intuition indicates another, go with your intuition!

The Tarot, Past Lives and Karma

Determining whether a Tarot spread refers to past life connections or karma is a subtle *and* obvious art. Subtle, because your intuition will alert you to (and/or confirm) a past life or karmic connection. Obvious, because certain Tarot cards in a spread will indicate that a past life or karmic connection is a possibility. As you continue to work with the cards and become more experienced with them, you will notice more and more, that your intuition will direct your attention to a past life-karmic situation in a consultation.

Determining past life-karmic connections requires practice, patience and actively connecting to and using your intuition.

These guidelines will help you to develop a stronger, more accurate, intuitive connection to the past life-karmic energy and information available to you in the tarot spreads you read.

And remember, **these are only guidelines, not hard and fast rules.** Use these guidelines to help you develop your own inner "radar" for finding and interpreting past life-karmic energy.

How to Conduct a Tarot Consultation

GUIDELINES:

Whenever you're considering the presence of past life-karmic energy in a spread or question, it's a good idea to reflect on the energy or influence of any Major Arcana card in the spread because the 22 cards of the Major Arcana represent the over-view, the perspective of God or the gods, a higher authority and/or something outside our immediate control. .

ALL MAJOR ARCANA ESPECIALLY:

THE HIGH PRIESTESS – She is endless and ageless; transformation

THE EMPEROR - Divine or Higher Power; God

THE HIEROPHANT – Divine messenger; old soul; Divine Teacher

THE HANGED MAN - "Divine delay"; karmic and past life issues; unresolved matters; people, habits, situations and circumstances from the past that hold one back

DEATH – transformation; death and re-birth; the end of a chapter in life; karma; all forms of passion—lust, anger, joy, hatred; vengeance; uncovering hidden information; resurrection; repentance; inheritance; legacies

DEVIL – old patterns; deep-rooted habits; past associations; vengeance; karma; feeling bound and enslaved; all forms of passion

THE MOON - the past; karma; record keeping; foundation of the soul; memories; deep, old or hidden issues

JUDGEMENT – transformation; death and re-birth; the end of a chapter in life; karma; consequences; accountability; uncovering hidden information; the necessity to be honest with one's self; resurrection; the voice of conscience; repentance; inheritance; legacies

AND TO A LESSER EXTENT:

THE LOVERS - the responsibility of choosing clearly from a new or current perspective; old choices; consequences; a need to unite the old with the new

THE CHARIOT – deep, old emotional issues (especially fear and anger); personal courage; inner conflict and struggle; a journey of personal development

STRENGTH - ego issues; fear or distrust of emotions—yours and/or others; emotional and/or creative blocks; the need to develop self-discipline and courage in order to deal with a particular person, type of person and/or issue

WHEEL OF FORTUNE – the "karmic wheel"; the need to enter a new phase of life; sudden changes in direction beyond our control; turning points; fate; destiny; a higher authority; inspiration from and direct experience with the Divine; religion; spirituality

JUSTICE – balance; the need for/to balance; ideals; idealism; higher truth; emotional contracts; karmic justice; hidden hostility; relationships

THE MINOR ARCANA:

Wands – inspirational; impassioned emotions; $E=mc^2$

Cups – flow; familiarity; the soul; past life feelings and emotions, recognition; ease;

Swords – reap results or consequences; instant familiarity

Pentacles – sow seeds; manifestation; familiar actions or habits

WANDS – especially the **3 of Wands**—following one's destiny; one's birthright; life cycles; life paths

4 of Wands – support from past life friends in this lifetime; one's 'tribe'

7 of Wands – need to move beyond the habits of the past and consciously choose a different soul path

8 of Wands – completion of past life quests; accrued spiritual 'points', help from one's 'tribe'

CUPS – especially the Ace of Cups—birth; rebirth; renewal

4 of Cups – the "old tapes"—habits and information from past lives; emotional past and foundation

8 of Cups – a necessary karmic passage; the need to let go of the old and move on

SWORDS – especially the 3 of Swords—self-inflicted pain caused by old past life belief systems, relationships and dogma

sometimes the 5 of Swords—past life fears influencing present circumstances

8 of Swords – the effects of old past life habits and stagnant past life belief systems and the need to move beyond them

9 of Swords – giving one's power to the accumulation of lifetimes of fear

10 of Swords – the end of a karmic situation

PENTACLES – especially the **Knight of Pentacles**—the continuity of life

sometimes the **3 of Pentacles**—creating and reaping from one's past life "vision"

4 of Pentacles – deeply rooted holding on and the need to change

5 of Pentacles – creating a positive present from past life experiences

6 of Pentacles – gifts, relationships and legacies from a past life

9 of Pentacles – the need to be rewarded and the reward for working beyond past life limitations

ALL 7's – the number '7' represents the spiritual path; Divine Direction

ALL 8's – the number '8' when it's on its side is the symbol for infinity and is related to karma and the laws of cause and effect

How to Conduct a Tarot Consultation

What to Do When You Draw a Blank

Sometimes, no matter how much you've studied, how much you know or how long you've been working with the cards, you're going to turn a card over, look at it and realize that you've drawn a blank. No, the card isn't blank, you're blank! You've just forgotten everything, you're unable to recall anything about the card.

It happens to everyone. No matter how well maintained your vehicle is, there are times when it just won't start. This is disconcerting enough when you're alone, but when a client is sitting across from you, it's a potential meltdown situation.

Rather than panic, though, breathe deeply, rhythmically, gently, look at your client and smile. Then pick up the card and begin to describe it to her/him.

"This is the 6 of Swords. It depicts a person on a boat who is being carried to a new place by someone or something more powerful than him or her. The person being carried is dressed in white, indicating purity and they're wearing a purple cloak, indicating Divine protection. This person is very calm and... "

By the time you get that far in describing the card, the intuitive doors will open, the perceptive window shades will go up and you'll once again be able to see and hear what the card is telling you.

After the client has gone, shuffle the cards and hold them to your heart—this will solidify the bond you have with them. Sit with them a few minutes and thank the cards, thank yourself and thank Divine Presence for your skills, talents and connections to the ethereal realms.

How to Conduct a Tarot Consultation

Getting To Know Your Tarot Cards

Exercise 1

Know Thyself: Best and Least Liked Tarot Cards

Whether you're new to the Tarot or familiar with it, this 10-minute exercise is a great way to get in tune with yourself and the cards. Look through all of the cards and choose the card you like or resonate with the most and the card you dislike or fear the most. Write your feelings about these two cards on this worksheet. Do this exercise once a week and notice how the cards, you and your relationship with them are changing.

How to Conduct a Tarot Consultation

Date _____

The Tarot Card I Like Best Is:

I Like This Tarot Card Best Because:

When I Look At This Tarot Card I Feel:

This Tarot Card Reminds Me Of:

****

The Tarot Card I Like Least Is:

I Like This Tarot Card Least Because:

When I Look At This Tarot Card I Feel:

This Tarot Card Reminds Me Of:

How to Conduct a Tarot Consultation

My Life Path Number and Life Guidance Tarot Card

My Life Path Number Is _____

My Life Guidance Tarot Card Is: _____

The month I was born (in numbers)_____

The date I was born _____

The year I was born (all 4 numbers) _____

Equals_____

Now add each number from the above total:

____ + ____ + ____ + ____ = _____

If you get a double digit number, add those: ____ + ____ = _____

The resulting single digit is your Life Path number. The Major Arcana Tarot card that matches your Life Path number is your Life Guidance card.

How to Conduct a Tarot Consultation

Example:

The month I was born (in numbers)	**4**
The date I was born	**7**
The year I was born (all 4 numbers)	**1985**
Equals	**1996**

Now add each number together from the above total:
1 + 9 + 9 + 6 = 25

If you get a double digit number, add those: 2 + 5 = 7

My Life Path Number Is: 7

My Life Guidance Tarot Card Is: The Chariot

❦

This Tarot Card's Message Regarding My Life Path Is:

How to Conduct a Tarot Consultation

Reading the Cards

Although there are many ways to become acquainted with your cards, I find that this method sharpens your conscious **and** your subconscious abilities at the same time. It really heightens your levels of perception as it helps you 'get' what each card is about number-wise, color-wise and every other way, as well. This method of acquainting yourself with the cards is an all senses assimilation and you'll be amazed at how quickly you get the gist of the Tarot.

In addition to your Tarot deck, you'll need a pen and a notebook. Your notebook will become an invaluable aid to your learning to work with the cards. You'll also be creating your own personal GPS system through the mystical land of Tarot.

Separate the Major Arcana cards from the Minor Arcana cards. Always count the Major Arcana cards to make sure you have all 22 in one stack. (It almost always happens that you've left at least one of the Major Arcana cards in the Minor Arcana stack!).

Separate the Minor Arcana cards by number. Put all 1's together, all 2's together, all 3's together. Do this with all of the numbers until you have 10 separate groups of cards.

Take the Court cards and put all of the **PAGES** with the 1's, PAGES have a '1' vibration. Put all of the **KNIGHTS** with the 3's, the KNIGHTS are the 12th card in each suit. The number 12 adds up to 3 numerologically (1+2=3). Put all of the **QUEENS** with the 4's, the QUEENS are the 13th card in each suit. The number 13 adds up to 4 numerologically (1+3=4). Put all of the **KINGS** with the 5's, the KINGS are the 14th card in each suit. The number 14 adds up to 5 numerologically (1+4=5).

How to Conduct a Tarot Consultation

Next, take the Major Arcana cards and put all **1's, THE MAGICIAN, THE WHEEL OF FORTUNE and THE SUN**, with the 1's of the Minor Arcana. Put all **2's, HIGH PRIESTESS, JUSTICE and JUDGEMENT**, with the 2's of the Minor Arcana. Put all **3's, THE EMPRESS, HANGED MAN and THE WORLD**, with the 3's of the Minor Arcana. Put all **4's, THE EMPEROR and DEATH**, with the 4's of the Minor Arcana. Put all **5's, THE HIEROPHANT and TEMPERANCE**, with the 5's of the Minor Arcana. Put all **6's, THE LOVERS and THE DEVIL**, with the 6's of the Minor Arcana. Put all **7's, THE CHARIOT and THE TOWER**, with the 7's of the Minor Arcana. Put all **8's, STRENGTH and THE STAR**, with the 8's of the Minor Arcana. Put all **9's, THE HERMIT and THE MOON**, with the 9's of the Minor Arcana.

Starting with the Minor Arcana, take the four 1's and put them side by side. Notice what is similar about all of the 1's. Now notice what is dis-similar about the 1's. Write your impressions in your notebook.

Leaving the 1's on the table in front of you, take the PAGES and place them in a row below the 1's. Notice what is similar and dis-similar about all of the PAGES. Compare them to the 1's. How are they like the 1's? Write your impressions in your notebook.

Leaving the 1's and the PAGES on the table in front of you, take THE MAGICIAN, THE WHEEL OF FORTUNE and THE SUN and place them in a row below the PAGES. Notice what is similar and dis-similar about them. Compare them to the 1's and the PAGES. How are they like the 1's and the PAGES? Write your impressions in your notebook.

Do this for the rest of the numbers. If you get stuck (and you will get stuck), relax and distract yourself for a few minutes, then go back to the cards. Don't try to absorb all of the numbers in one sitting. If

How to Conduct a Tarot Consultation

you study one or two numbers a night, you'll give yourself time to integrate them into your system.

The FOOL is unique. It has no number and is usually referred to as 'Key 0'. Study the FOOL by itself and with each of the number combinations. Notice what he tells you about each of the cards and numbers. Notice what he tells you about himself. Write your impressions in your notebook.

Once you've gone through all nine numbers, go back to the 1's and start the process again. Each time you do this exercise, you'll notice something new and you'll retain more and more about the Tarot.

Working with the Cards

The more interaction you have with your Tarot cards, the better you'll be able to know them. In addition to the previous exercises, these two will keep you engaged with the Tarot on a daily basis.

The first one is the **My Tarot Cards for the Month and Day.** In the **Tarot Spreads and Charts** chapter, you'll find a **My Tarot Cards for the Month and Day** chart. Copy the chart and record your daily cards on it.

On the first day of the month, pull a card from your deck. That card represents the energy of the coming month for you. Write the name of the card at the top of the chart in the space provided. Then, pull a card for that first day of the month. That card represents the energy of the day for you. Write the name of that card in the space provided for it on the chart. Thereafter, each day, pull a card from the deck for that day and record it on the chart.

How to Conduct a Tarot Consultation

You can pull the card on the morning of the day or at bedtime, the night before the day.

I pull my card for the next day on the night before because mornings can be hectic and I often have to hurry to begin my day. Pulling my daily card the night before gives me time to contemplate the card's energy and write my impressions of it in my journal or notebook. An added advantage of pulling my daily card the night before, I can "sleep on it", that is, I'll have time to subconsciously process the card's energy while I sleep and when I awake, the card and I are in sync with each other. Being in sync with the card's energy gives me more understanding and power in how the energy of the card plays out in my life during that day.

The second exercise will show you what energies are at work in your life for the calendar year. Knowledge is power and the more you know about your life, the more you'll be able to take advantage of the energy available to you.

This exercise is called **My Major Arcana Tarot Card Teachers for the Year.** In the Tarot Spreads and Charts chapter, you'll find a My Major Arcana Tarot Card Teachers for the Year form. Each year, copy the form and record your Major Arcana Teachers cards on it.

Separate the Major Arcana cards from the Minor Arcana cards and put the Minor Arcana cards off to the side, you won't be using them in this exercise. Remember, always count the Major Arcana cards to make sure you have all 22 in one stack. (It almost always happens that you've left at least one of the Major Arcana cards in the Minor Arcana stack!).

Shuffle the Major Arcana cards and place them face down on a table in three rows. With your left hand, pick the card that represents

How to Conduct a Tarot Consultation

your spiritual or inner lessons teacher for the year. Don't turn it over, yet. Set it to the side and with your right hand, pick the card that represents your worldly or outer lessons teacher for the year.

Now, turn both cards over and record the cards and your impressions of them on the form. If you pick a card or cards you don't like for your yearly teachers, this is a great opportunity to "make lemonade out of lemons." Remember, each card holds a positive, neutral and negative energy. How you deal with the energies makes all the difference.

My friends and I pick our Major Arcana teachers every year (or rather, they pick us!). For seven out of ten years, I picked the Hanged Man as one of my teachers. It got so that the others would joke when I arrived at the ceremony. Remarks like, *"Where's your boyfriend? Oh, that's right, he's on the table waiting for you to pick him again,"* were pretty common. I laughed along with them as I secretly prayed that I wouldn't have to endure another year of his limitations.

About six months into the fourth straight year of having the Hanged Man as one of my teachers, I surrendered and finally stopped resisting. If the card kept showing up for me, I obviously had something to learn from it.

The most amazing things began to happening! All of the delayed projects I'd been trying to actualize started manifesting. They manifested in their own ways and not in the ways I'd been trying to make them happen. As I stepped out of the way and listened to and followed Divine instructions, I witnessed and participated in a series of effortless wins.

Well, who knew!? Finally, I understood why the Hanged Man is called the card of 'Divine Delay.' Until I surrendered to the Hanged

How to Conduct a Tarot Consultation

Man's energy and witnessed the results, I thought 'Divine Delay' meant 'never.' After I surrendered, it was clearly demonstrated to me that it meant, *"MY way, not your way."* We do have opposable thumbs and the capacity to choose but we don't have a better plan than God. My years with the Hanged Man as one of my teachers taught me to relax and trust that there was a better way. Now, when the Hanged Man appears in one of my readings, I'm as calm, patient and assured as the person on the card and I no longer pray for him to go away.

When you pick your spiritual or inner teacher card **don't** put it back in with the other unpicked Major Arcana cards. Always put it to the side and turn it over after you've picked your spiritual or inner lessons teacher card. That way, you won't get confused if something distracts you while you're in the process of picking your cards.

One year, my friends and I weren't able to get together and have our annual party/ Major Arcana Teachers ceremony, so we all agreed to pick our teachers on our own. About noon the next day, I got a phone call from Doreene, a very dear friend and colleague. She didn't sound distressed but I could tell she wasn't her usual calm self. She told me that right after she'd picked her spiritual or inner teacher card, she'd gotten distracted by a neighbor and had looked at the card as she absent mindedly put it back with the rest of the Major Arcana cards.

After the neighbor left, she chose her worldly or outer teacher card. That's when her calmness began to desert her. She had chosen the same card for her spiritual or inner teacher and her worldly or outer teacher and that card was the Death card! She knew that it didn't mean she would actually physically die, but she was worried about the enormity of the transformation that would come into her life as a result of both teachers being represented by the intense energy of the Death card. She did have an intense year and her life did radically change, fortunately, it was all positive and profitable.

And we both learned a huge lesson from her experience, never put the first card back into the deck until after you've picked the second card! I gladly pass this lesson on to you, with the hope that you will heed it.

What about do-overs? Suppose you pick a card or cards you don't like as your yearly teachers. It should be alright to put it back and pick another one, shouldn't it? In a word—NO. The Universe knows what you need and the Universe knows what you originally picked. And that's the experience the Universe is going to provide you with.

At one of the Major Arcana Teachers ceremonies, my friend, Bette, and I didn't like our cards and we decided to put them back and pick something that we felt was more representative of who we were. We reasoned that the cards were just pieces of colored paper and that it was us who put the meaning into the ceremony and not the cards. *Ahh— denial, what a lovely cruise down a non-existent river!*

Since we'd both picked the Fool and the Tower, we made sure we picked cards that were more to our liking. (Yes, that means we peeked!) I chose the Empress and the Sun and Bette chose something equally idyllic. We agreed to keep in touch and share our stories of how well the year was going for us.

Our year progressed smoothly until Bette, who was from New York, made an obligatory family visit to the city. She'd left her birthplace because she didn't like it, didn't like being there and never wanted to live there again. On this trip, for whatever reason, Bette fell in love with New York! She knew she had to live there again, so she rushed back to L.A., hastily packed her things and moved back to her birthplace.

It all happened so fast that we didn't have time to talk much about it. I was a bit distracted anyway, because I was preparing to leave for a two-week vacation in England.

While meditating in the inner circle of Stonehenge one evening, I received a message that I was to leave L.A. and move to England within the next five weeks! Which I did. Before that meditation, moving to England had never crossed my mind. It was a most amazing sojourn and I learned a lot on that eleven and a half month long pilgrimage.

If Bette and I hadn't been so willful, we'd have been better prepared for the huge surprise that awaited us. Instead, we chose to ignore the teachers and their teachings. We both learned something important through this experience and I'm passing it on to you.

You really don't choose the lessons; the lessons choose you. No matter what you think about the cards you pick, there is an important and necessary lesson or message in them for you. Denying the messenger doesn't cancel the message.

Keeping It Simple

Although learning to interpret the messages the cards have for you seems like and is a time intensive task, actually interpreting the messages doesn't have to be.

It is important to learn about the cards, that's how you get to know what they're capable of saying without a lot of angst. I liken learning about the cards and finally being able to effortlessly interpret them to learning to drive a car and easily driving it.

The first time I took a driving lesson, the instructor told me that driving was simple. In order to properly drive a car, all I had to do was simultaneously, look through my windshield and pay attention to the traffic around me while looking through the rear window and the windshield of the car in front of me and noticing what was happening there, while at the same time pay attention to what I could see in my two side mirrors as I checked my rearview mirror to see, not only the car behind me, but through that car's windshield and rear window as well—all the while keeping both hands on the steering wheel and driving safely!

I looked at him in disbelief and told him that doing all of that at the same time was impossible. He assured me it wasn't and even though he expressed confidence in my being able to learn, I realized right then that I was in over my head. At that moment, I only wanted one thing, to get out of the car and renew my previously life-long commitment to helping subsidize taxi cabs.

I didn't, though. I stuck with it and passed my driving exam two weeks later on the first try. With repetitious practice, the impossible became the possible which finally became something so natural that I don't even think about it now, I just do it.

And that's what interpreting the cards will be like for you if you work with them on a regular basis. At first you're trying to remember all of the seemingly impossible to know information, but with repetitious practice, you get comfortable with it, and what comes comfortably becomes natural and what is natural just happens without thinking about it.

When my students first come to my classes, I don't tell them what they don't know, I support them in discovering that they do know. We are a visual species and inside everyone is the ability to consciously interpret the visual messages we receive. While I respect the fact that

How to Conduct a Tarot Consultation

they are new to the Tarot, I don't view them as novices. Because I don't view them as novices, they stop believing that it's difficult or impossible for them to accurately interpret the cards. And because they no longer see their abilities in a negative light, when called upon, they simply read the cards, accurately, profoundly, insightfully.

And you can, too. Especially in the beginning, always start with a question or issue. When interpreting the messages in the cards, **always** keep the question or issue in mind. Then look at the cards, the scene or action in them will begin to clearly reveal the story. And listen to your inner voice. Out of the blue, does a particular song come to mind? Are you suddenly reminded of a certain incident or type of person? Are you feeling happy, sad, ill at ease?

All of these elements have come together at that time for a reason. Take a deep, rhythmic, gentle breath and start talking, even when you're by yourself. As you begin to speak, the story (which has been waiting to be told) begins to tell itself. If you get a feeling about something, ask your client about it. Ask them if the song or whatever has come to mind means anything to them.

At first, speaking to your client about what you see will seem daunting, but be cautiously courageous. Nobody is right 100% of the time, but you can get pretty close. You have to be willing to be wrong if you're going to learn how and what it takes to be right. With time and practice, you can learn to be insightfully accurate 95-100% of the time.

Knowing the stated meaning of a card or suit is a good thing, it'll provide a spring board for your intuition. Believing that it's the only meaning for a card or suit is not a good thing; a belief can be a cause for stagnation and blindness.

How to Conduct a Tarot Consultation

The Cups traditionally refer to happiness and well-being. A client once asked me about her brother. She wanted to know how well he was doing. I used the Process Spread and the heart of the matter was the Ace of Cups and the foundation card was the 10 of Cups.

Tradition would insist that her brother was doing really well, but my heart was heavy as I looked at a spread I'd have been happy to have for myself. I told my client that her brother was not doing well at all; that he'd fallen back into his old habits and I felt there might be a substance abuse issue.

She then revealed to me that she'd had a feeling he was drinking again. After only two weeks of being out of re-hab for alcohol abuse, he was showing signs of his old addictive behavior. If I'd have gone with the traditional Tarot belief system, I'd have wrongly assured her that her brother was fine. Of course there were Cups—he was drinking again! Living proof that Cups aren't always a sign of glad tidings.

Another client came to me because she'd finally met "the one." She was sure of it. They really hit it off and things were progressing smoothly. She wanted confirmation from me that this relationship was really worth her investment of feelings, time and energy.

I used the Process Spread again and the majority of the cards were Pentacles with the heart of the matter being the 8 of Pentacles. As I looked at the cards, I felt pretty good about her relationship. I lifted my eyes from the cards to tell her the good news and she burst out crying! I was shocked and frightened, what could have happened in the minute I'd looked away from her to interpret the spread!?

"Oh no!" she wailed, "they're all Pentacles; there are no Cups! If there are no Cups, it can't really be love!" Regaining my composure, I took her hands in mine and I looked her in the eyes and said, *"You already know that you love each other, you don't need cards for that. You want it to last, don't you?"* She uttered a sheepish, *"Oh,"* as she nodded her head and stopped crying.

I asked her about her reaction to the spread and she told me that she'd recently read a Tarot book that emphatically stated that Cups had to be present in the spread in order for a relationship to be meaningful. This experience proved two things to me. One, a little knowledge can be a dangerous thing, and two, I was right to go with my feelings and not some belief system simply because it was part of a tradition.

Start practicing with the **1-CARD READING.** Begin your interpretations with, *"I feel"* instead of *"I think"* and write your questions and interpretations on the form. It's amazing what one card can tell you—that one card is often proof that *"a picture is worth a thousand words."*

A few years ago, I was doing consultations at Malibu Shaman Bookstore, a wonderful metaphysical shop in Malibu, California. From where I sat, I had a direct eye line to the front door and I could see everyone who came into the shop. One lovely Sunday afternoon, I noticed a man standing in the doorway. At first glance, he just didn't seem the type to frequent a place like the Shaman. From his energy and the way he was dressed, I thought he was lost.

He entered the store and as he walked toward me, I took note of his expensive but well-worn cowboy boots, the custom, hand tooled brown leather belt with the big silver buckle that snaked through the belt loops on his jeans, the neatly tucked in plaid cowboy shirt that emphasized his ample girth, his impressive Stetson El Patron cowboy hat, the way he walked with a rolling gait that spoke of his having spent much of his life on a horse and his piercing no-nonsense gaze.

How to Conduct a Tarot Consultation

Although he looked like a hard-working cowboy, I could sense that there was a lot more to him than that. As he got closer to me, I could also sense that something memorable was about to take place.

He sat in the chair opposite me and after introductions, he told me in his Southwestern drawl, that he knew I could help him because, *"You've got the look."* I'd heard that before, and I encouraged him to continue. *"Well,"* he said in that deliberate way men from that part of the country speak, *"I've got a daughter, my only child."* And I knew immediately that she resembled him in appearance—pleasant but plain with an ample build.

"She's met this fella and he's proposed to her. I want my baby girl to be happy, I just want to make sure she's picked the right fella." I knew what that meant, too. He was worried that this 'fella' was too handsome, too ardent and too much of a smooth talker and that he might be after his 'baby girl's' inheritance.

I shuffled the cards of the original Mythic Tarot deck, fanned them out on the table and asked him to pick one with his left hand. (I find that the left hand is great for choosing cards that reveal secrets.)

He reached over, picked a card and turned it over. It was the Knight of Wands! If ever there was a card depicting a handsome, smooth-talking, red convertible driving, motorcycle riding, pony tail wearing, black leather jacket sporting, tattooed bad boy, it was that particular Knight from that deck. We both stared at the card in stunned silence. Then we looked at each other. Not a word passed between us (I half expected to hear the jingle of spurs and the sound track to the film classic, "High Noon"). Finally, he stood up and politely said, *"Thank you ma'am, I've got some work to do back home,"* and he left.

The theater of life is never boring and that session was more than enough proof of that fact. I never saw the client again, but I imagine that shortly thereafter, somewhere in the panhandle, there was a smooth-talking bad boy running for the hills.

With the **3-CARD SPREAD (LINEAR)**, you'll get a bigger sense of what's going on and learn to blend the information of the three cards into a cohesive message. Use the suggestions for different ways to phrase your questions as a guide. You'll be amazed at how quickly you get comfortable with the interpretation process. Remember to record your interpretations on this form, too.

Clarifying Cards

A clarifying card is a card that is pulled to help you better understand an individual card in the spread or the entire spread. They can shed more light on the card, the querent, the issue and/or the spread.

Please don't over-do it, though. At the most, two or three clarifying cards are enough to help you decipher the clues in the other cards. Any more cards than that and you're right back in muddled confusion.

If the clarifying cards aren't helping you to clarify the message, you probably need to re-think the question and approach the answer from a different perspective.

How to Conduct a Tarot Consultation

Your Mission

When a client comes to you for advice and counseling, they're almost always in a vulnerable state. Please remember that you are the bridge that can connect them to either hope, strength and possibility or to despair, negativity and depression.

You must tell your client the truth, but you have to do it in a way that empowers and supports them. If you get the message that your client has a tough road ahead of them, listen for guidance as to what the meaning of the experience is for the client and their evolution. We're a resilient species and if we can understand the meaning behind the experience, we can go through it with awareness, hope and grace.

Too many times, people in our profession are the purveyors of doom and gloom. They 'see' that something potentially intense is going to happen to the client and they stop searching for any additional information as they then burden the client with the news and the heaviness of their situation. This approach to counseling doesn't serve anyone. You have the power to assist a client in turning their eyes to the endless possibilities of a star filled sky or the stifling darkness of a fathomless abyss. There is a meaning in every experience. Your job is to support your client by finding the meaning **and** the message and conveying it to them.

When a client tells you, *"You were right,"* that makes your ego feel good. When they tell you, *"You were right and you helped me so much,"* that makes both your ego and your heart feel good—**and** that experience of knowing you made a positive difference in someone's life is priceless.

Integrity

For the most part, I'm a pretty flexible person, willing to entertain the validity of a lot of different view-points. There are some exceptions, though.

When a client asks about health, you can choose to answer the question or do what a lot of practitioners do—tell them you don't answer questions about health. There are legal and ethical reasons for taking care in responding to the issue of health. You don't want to be the person they claim is responsible for dissuading them from seeking medical advice from a medical professional.

When asked about health issues, I always respond with these two statements before I say anything else, *"If you have health concerns, please discuss them with the health practitioners of your choice"* and then I ask, *"Why are you asking that question?"* Usually there isn't an issue and the client is just curious about the general state of their health. Sometimes the issue is deeper than that and I re-state my advice to them about seeking help from the health practitioners of their choice. I then tell them that, if they want, I'm willing to look at the underlying spiritual meaning of their health issue. If they agree to that, then, that's what we do. If they don't agree to that, we move on to another subject.

Another big integrity issue involves questions related to death and dying. I suggest you avoid any predictions about this subject. There may be a practitioner out there who can accurately predict when a person is going to die. I'm glad I'm not that person. That's a type of responsibility that I don't think belongs to us; it's the province of a Higher Power.

When I'm asked a death and dying question, I respond with, *"There are three questions I don't answer. I don't know when anyone is going*

How to Conduct a Tarot Consultation

to be born, babies are often born at the most inconvenient times and in the most inconvenient places, like taxi-cabs. I don't know when anyone is going to die, only God knows that. And I don't know the winning lottery numbers, if I did, we'd be having this conversation on my yacht in the south of France."

This truthful and light hearted statement defines my boundaries, steers the session in the right direction and helps put the client in a relaxed frame of mind.

The United States is practically the only place in the world where just about everyone freaks out at the sight of the DEATH card. People from other countries understand that it is simply referring to transformation and change of some kind. When the DEATH card comes up during a session, I quickly and lightly say to my client, *"Don't worry, you still have to get up in the morning."* There's usually a relieved laugh at that little statement because it dispels much of their fear and defuses the situation. With the client at ease, the smooth flow of the consultation is once again on track.

"Is it alright to ask questions about someone else without getting their permission first?"

Yes.

You ask mutual acquaintances about other people all the time without telling them or getting their permission first—how they're doing; if they're still involved with their romantic partner; if they're still working at the same job; if their health is good; if they're still living in the same place; if they'd be interested in dating you.

Those are pretty much the same questions you'd ask about someone you're interested in during a Tarot or Intuitive session, too. A Tarot or Intuitive session is an information gathering experience, just like the chat with the mutual acquaintance. It provides you with an opportunity to gather information about someone or something you're interested in.

Some Tarot readers and Intuitive consultants disagree with that and consider it an invasive act if you ask about someone without getting their permission first. I don't.

You'll have to make up your own mind about that. If you think it's invasive and wrong to do, don't do it. If you think it's OK, then, do what I do—ask.

Reading the Tarot for Yourself

Many Tarot enthusiasts think it's wrong or impossible to read your own Tarot cards. Reading your own cards is one of the great perks of learning to navigate this wonderful, ancient information retrieval system. Just as with interpreting the cards for others, you can ask anything you want more information on; your own self-development, your relationship to some thing or someone else, which restaurant to dine in, what movie to see.

There is a trick to doing it successfully, though. The trick hinges on these three things: courage, self-honesty and a willingness to see things as they are and not just as you want them to be. In addition, you'll need to employ the following steps:

1 - Objectivity: In order to get information that will be useful to you, you'll have to learn to be objective about the answers you get. In order to do that, you'll have to learn to move past your emotions, which is not the same thing as setting your emotions aside. I don't really know how do-able it is to set your emotions aside about something that's important to you. We are an emotional species and filtering events and information through our emotions is part of how we're wired. You can learn to move past them temporarily, though.

2 - Simplicity: Remember to write out your question, issue or concern. Keep your Tarot spreads simple, using 1 to 5 cards per question, that way your thinking processes are less likely to be immediately engaged or activated. Lay the cards out face down and leave them that way until you've laid out all of the cards in the spread. Take a deep breath, slowly exhale and quickly turn all of the cards over.

3 - Quickness: Now, take a quick look at your spread. Without thinking or trying to figure out what the spread or the cards mean, immediately write down your first impressions. After you've written them down, re-read your question and go over the spread, one card at a time. Write those observations down, too.

What you're trying to do is get out of your own emotional way so that you can have a clear sight-line to the answers to your questions. The first quick look is that briefly open window that can provide you with the objectivity and clarity you need to be able to effectively read the Tarot cards for yourself.

Read for yourself on a daily basis. The more you practice this method, the easier you'll find it to be to read, interpret and get the messages your cards are happy to deliver to you. You'll also discover that you're becoming more objective and more in control of your emotions in the other aspects of your life, too.

10

Tarot Spreads and Charts

An accurate Tarot reading helps to solve the mysteries of life, and as with all mysteries, it's the clues and the interpretation of those clues that are the keys to getting your answers.

The Tarot cards are the clues that provide the answers; the Tarot spreads are the maps that tell you what story is being told and how to accurately read the clues that will reveal the most direct path to the answers to your questions. Like all good maps, a good Tarot spread shows you where you are, how you got there, what the topography is like, and how to get to where you want to go.

A good Tarot spread is a priceless ally. When cards are laid out in a spread, a story line with themes, meanings and characters is revealed. The weaving of this story and the perspective gained from it are essential to the art of accurate interpretation.

In this chapter, you'll find all kinds of Tarot spreads that will help guide you in your quest for the answers to your questions about life—relationships, security, spirituality and all of the areas in between.

As you work with them, you may feel the need to make your own changes to them, please feel free to do so. As I've said many times before, the Intuitive Arts and its processes are part of an experiential realm, as you progress and adapt to them, they must, in turn, adapt to you. It's a good idea to make copies of the original spreads for future use.

Tarot Spreads and Charts

Make copies of the **My Tarot Cards for the Month and Day** chart for future use. On the first day of the month, pull a card from your deck. That card represents the energy of the coming month for you. Write the name of the card at the top of the chart in the space provided. Then, pull a card for that first day of the month. That card represents the energy of the day for you. Write the name of that card in the space provided for it on the chart. Thereafter, each day, pull a card from the deck for that day and record it on the chart.

My Tarot Cards for the Month and Day

Month & Year: _____ Card: _____

SUNDAY	MONDAY	TUESDAY	WEDNESDAY	THURSDAY	FRIDAY	SATURDAY

Week 1

_____

Week 2

_____

Week 3

_____

Week 4

_____

Week 5

_____

Observations:

Make copies of the **My Major Arcana Tarot Card Teachers for the Year** form for future use. Each year, record your Major Arcana Teachers cards on it.

Separate the Major Arcana cards from the Minor Arcana cards and put the Minor Arcana cards off to the side, you won't be using them in this exercise. Remember, always count the Major Arcana cards to make sure you have all 22 in one stack.

Shuffle the Major Arcana cards and place them face down on a table in three rows. With your left hand, pick the card that represents your spiritual or inner lessons teacher for the year. Don't turn it over, yet. Set it to the side and with your right hand, pick the card that represents your worldly or outer lessons teacher for the year.

Now, turn both cards over and record the cards and your impressions of them on the form.

Tarot Spreads and Charts

MY MAJOR ARCANA TAROT CARD TEACHERS FOR 20____

My Spiritual/Inner Teacher is Represented By:

I Feel My Major Spiritual Lesson This Year Is:

****

My Worldly/Outer Teacher Is Represented By:

I Feel My Major Worldly Lesson This Year Is:

****

I Feel My Combined Spiritual and Worldly Lessons This Year Can Teach Me:

1 - Card Reading

The **1-CARD READING** is great for taking the measure of any situation. It's amazing what one card can tell you. That one card is often proof that *"a picture is worth a thousand words."*

1 - Card Reading

Question: Name
                                             Date
                                             Time
Feelings or Interpretations: Deck

Created by Sheilaa Hite

3 - Card Spread (Linear)

This linear 3-card spread can be used to answer a variety of questions and to shed light on many different issues. You can "create" this spread any way you want in order to receive the information you're seeking.

Each card represents an aspect of the answer to your question. First, decide which of the ten spreads best relates to your query, and then, moving from left to right, name each position according to the number sequence, i.e., "card 1 represents; card 2 represents; card 3 represents". As you lay the cards out in this order with the appropriate position titles, you will see your answers unfold before you! Make copies of the blank spread for future use.

* * * *Listed here are suggestions to get you started.* * * *
Add to the list as you think of other questions and issues you seek answers to

1 - BEGINNING ~ MIDDLE ~ END

2 - NEGATIVE ~ NEUTRAL ~ POSITIVE

3 - BODY ~ MIND ~ SPIRIT

4 - SUBCONSCIOUS ~ CONSCIOUS ~ SUPERCONSCIOUS

5 - OPTION #1 ~ OPTION #2 ~ OPTION #3

6 - WORST CASE SCENARIO ~ NEUTRAL ~ BEST CASE SCENARIO

3 - Card Spread - Linear

Question: Name
                                                   Date
                                                   Time
Feelings or Interpretations: Deck

| 1) | 2) | 3) |

Created by Sheilaa Hite

7 - DISADVANTAGES OF THIS COURSE OF ACTION ~ TRUE NATURE OF THIS COURSE OF ACTION ~ ADVANTAGES OF THIS COURSE OF ACTION

8 - WHAT IS BEHIND ME (THE PAST) ~ WHERE I STAND NOW (THE PRESENT) ~ WHAT IS BEFORE ME (THE FUTURE)

9 - THE HIDDEN ISSUES IN THIS RELATIONSHIP ~ THE TRUE NATURE OF THIS RELATIONSHIP ~ WHERE THIS RELATIONSHIP IS HEADED

*** *This last 3-card (linear) spread—#10—is excellent for gaining perspective in any situation by answering the question:*
WHAT'S HAPPENING NOW?

10 - THE NATURE OF THE PRESENT SITUATION ~ MY (or OTHERS) ATTITUDE TOWARD THIS SITUATION ~ THE MAIN THING TO KEEP IN MIND REGARDING THIS SITUATION

Tarot Spreads and Charts

Chalice

The **Chalice Spread** is powerful, informative and really brings out your intuitive abilities. The positions aren't numbered. Think of the 'bowl' part as a container. What does it hold? Think of the 'stem' part as a support. Is it strong or weak? Does it/can it support the 'bowl'? Make copies of the blank form for future use.

Chalice Spread

Question:

Feelings or Interpretations:

Name
Date
Time
Deck

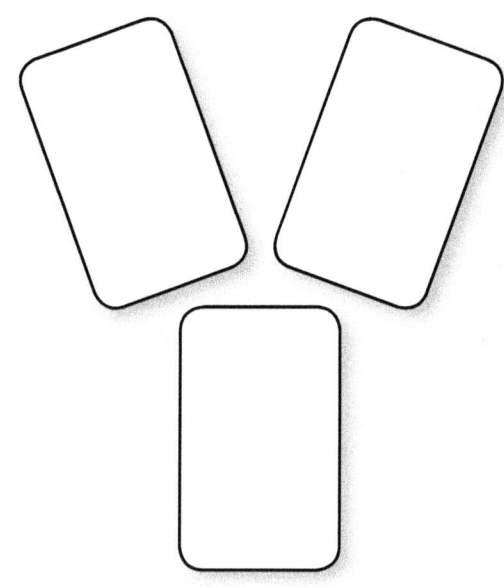

Created by Sheilaa Hite

Dream Interpretation

The **Dream Interpretation** spread will help you decipher the often mysterious clues given to you in your dreams. Separate the Major Arcana cards from the Minor Arcana and pick the Major Arcana card for position 1, first. Then shuffle both Arcanas together and pick the remaining cards. Make copies of the blank form for future use.

Dream Interpretation Spread

Question: Name
                                                 Date
                                                 Time
Feelings or Interpretations: Deck

3) What does this dream want me to know?

4) Why was the message given to me this way?

1) Major Arcana

Is this a valid message?

5) What action do I take now?

2) Is this valid message referring to the material realm?

Created by Sheilaa Hite and Linda Farmer

Personal Power

The **Personal Power Spread** is both specific and versatile. Ask the question, "What is my Personal Power this lifetime?" and you'll get an understanding of how you best operate in life. Ask, "What is my Personal Power in this situation?" and you'll get an excellent picture of your power in that situation. Make copies of the blank form for future use.

Personal Power Spread

Question: Name
                                         Date
                                         Time
Feelings or Interpretations: Deck

3) Logical mind, Consciousness

2) Intuition, Subconscious

4) Physical expression, outcome, lesson

6) Heart of the Matter

1) Message from the Universe

5) Spiritual expression, outcome, lesson

Created by Sheilaa Hite

I Am

The **I Am** spread is such an important spread because it clearly shows you who you are and how the Divine Power sees you as opposed to what you've come to believe about yourself. Use it in different situations to understand how to best use your power. Separate the Major Arcana cards from the Minor Arcana and use the Major Arcana cards only for this spread. Make copies of the blank form for future use.

I Am Spread - Major Arcana

Question: Name
                                                   Date
                                                   Time
Feelings or Interpretations: Deck

Major Arcana

Who I think I am

Major Arcana

Who I really am

Created by Sheilaa Hite

Relationship

The **Relationship Spread.** I don't have to tell you what this one's about. Everyone is interested in relationships—romantic, platonic, professional, familial. Use this spread to answer those age-old questions. Separate the Major Arcana cards from the Minor Arcana and pick the Major Arcana card for the center position first. Then shuffle both Arcanas together and pick the remaining cards. Make copies of the blank form for future use.

Relationship Spread

Question: Name
                                           Date
                                           Time
Feelings or Interpretations: Deck

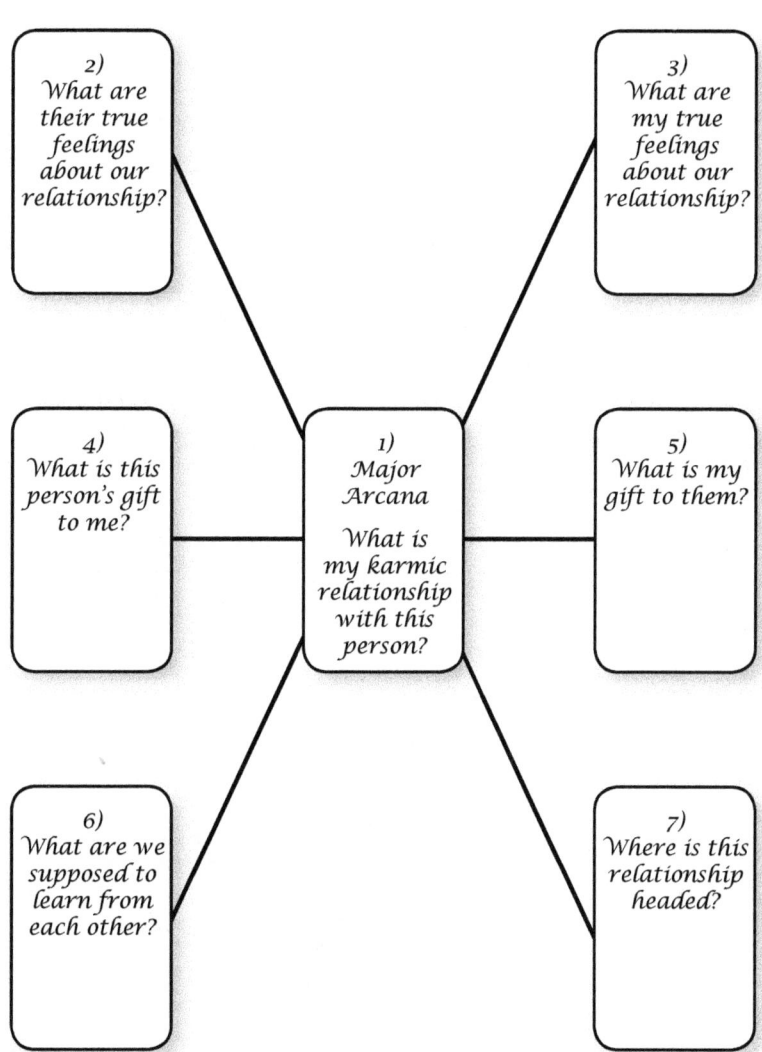

Created by Sheilaa Hite

Process

The **Process Spread** is the workhorse spread of the group. I use it for almost all of my in depth questions and issues. It's a truly organic spread, it shows you the stationary and changing dynamics of the situation and the people involved on all levels. Make copies of the blank form for future use

The Process Spread

Question: Name
                                                       Date
                                                       Time
Feelings or Interpretations: Deck

	Querent; Question; Subject	
	Heart of the Matter	
Behind the scenes; What's hidden; What pushes the matter forward	Clarifies/ Supports Heart of the Matter and Foundation	Probable result of the matter; Wild cards
	Foundation	

Created by Sheilaa Hite

Defining Moment

The **Defining Moment** spread is revealing, dynamic and transformational. A defining moment is a pivotal point in your development/life. It's the moment that makes you special as a result of having made an important choice or decision. Separate the Major Arcana cards from the Minor Arcana and pick the Major Arcana cards for positions 1, 5 and 8 first. Then shuffle both Arcanas together and pick the remaining cards. Make copies of the blank form for future use.

Defining Moment Spread

Question:
How can I consciously recognize, own and activate this defining moment?

Feelings or Interpretations:

Name
Date
Time
Deck

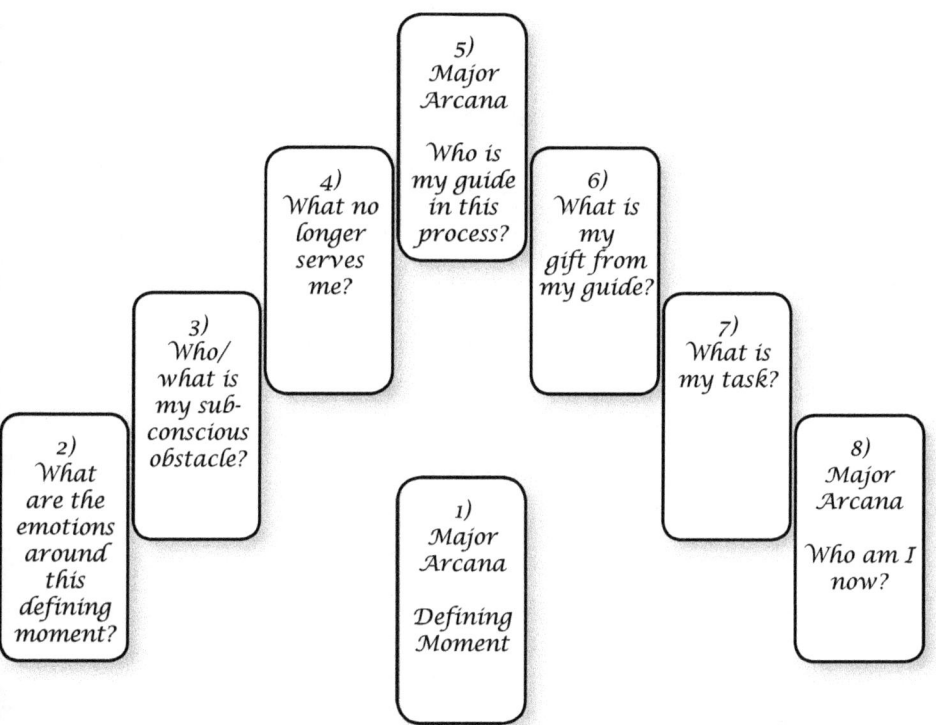

2) What are the emotions around this defining moment?

3) Who/what is my subconscious obstacle?

4) What no longer serves me?

5) Major Arcana — Who is my guide in this process?

6) What is my gift from my guide?

7) What is my task?

8) Major Arcana — Who am I now?

1) Major Arcana — Defining Moment

Created by Sheilaa Hite

Crossroads

The **Crossroads** spread is perfect for those times when you want more information on your choices and the results or consequences of those choices. Make copies of the blank form for future use.

Crossroads Spread

Question:

Feelings or Interpretations:

Name
Date
Time
Deck

5) Where this road leads

7) Where this road leads

4) What I will encounter if I continue on this road

6) What I will encounter if I take this different road

3) Where I am now

1) Heart of the Matter

2) What led me here

Created by Linda Farmer

Tower

The **Tower Spread** is aptly named because it comes in handy when you are dealing with or need to change. It has a way of showing you important aspects of the issue from subtle, unique perspectives. Make copies of the blank form for future use.

Tower Spread

Question: Name
                                                            Date
                                                            Time
Feelings or Interpretations: Deck

- Querent; Question; Subject
- Action you can take; Change you can make
- Guidance/Inspiration
- Who or what is creating an obstacle
- What is not obvious (good or bad)
- Past influences
- Question; Heart of the Matter
- Present influences

Created by Sheilaa Hite

Ripples in a Pond

The **Ripples in a Pond** spread is great when you're looking for the answers to questions that deal with the far-reaching effects of a decision or an action. Make copies of the blank form for future use.

Ripples in a Pond Spread

Question:

Feelings or Interpretations:

Name
Date
Time
Deck

| 4) Subtle or hidden long-term effects/results | 3) Hidden from view; Need to be aware of; Energy or action toward or against you | 1) Heart of the Matter Querent; Subject matter | 2) Environment; Others; Action required; Immediate effects | 5) Obvious long-term effects/results |

Created by Sheilaa Hite

Money Bags

The **Money Bags** spread is a great manifesting spread. Once you get a clear picture of what you need to do to activate and access your abundance in the ethereal realm, you'll be able to create it in the material realm. Separate the Major Arcana cards from the Minor Arcana and pick the Major Arcana cards for the three center positions inside the bag first. Then shuffle both Arcanas together and pick the remaining cards. Make copies of the blank form for future use.

Money Bags Spread

Question:

Feelings or Interpretations:

Name
Date
Time
Deck

3 Seeds – What's needed to activate your bounty

Major Arcana

What you can do to access your bounty

Major Arcana

Gold Nugget – What is hidden but was always there & will enhance and enrich the 3 Gifts

Major Arcana

3 Gifts – They are always paying dividends to you

Created by Sheilaa Hite

Spiral Revelations

The **Spiral Revelations** spread is a profoundly revealing and liberating spread. Spirals play an important role in nature, as well as in the spiritual, mythological and psychological development of human beings. The spiral works in both directions—spiraling inward and spiraling outward. If you want to learn about your process from an inner perspective, lay the cards out from the center Heart of the Matter position and begin your reading there and spiral outward to the last card, the Conscious Expression. If you want to know more about your process from a conscious or outer perspective, lay the cards out starting from the Conscious Expression position and spiral inward to the Heart of the Matter position. Make copies of the blank form for future use.

Spiral Revelations Spread

Question: Name
                                                   Date
                                                   Time
Feelings or Interpretations: Deck

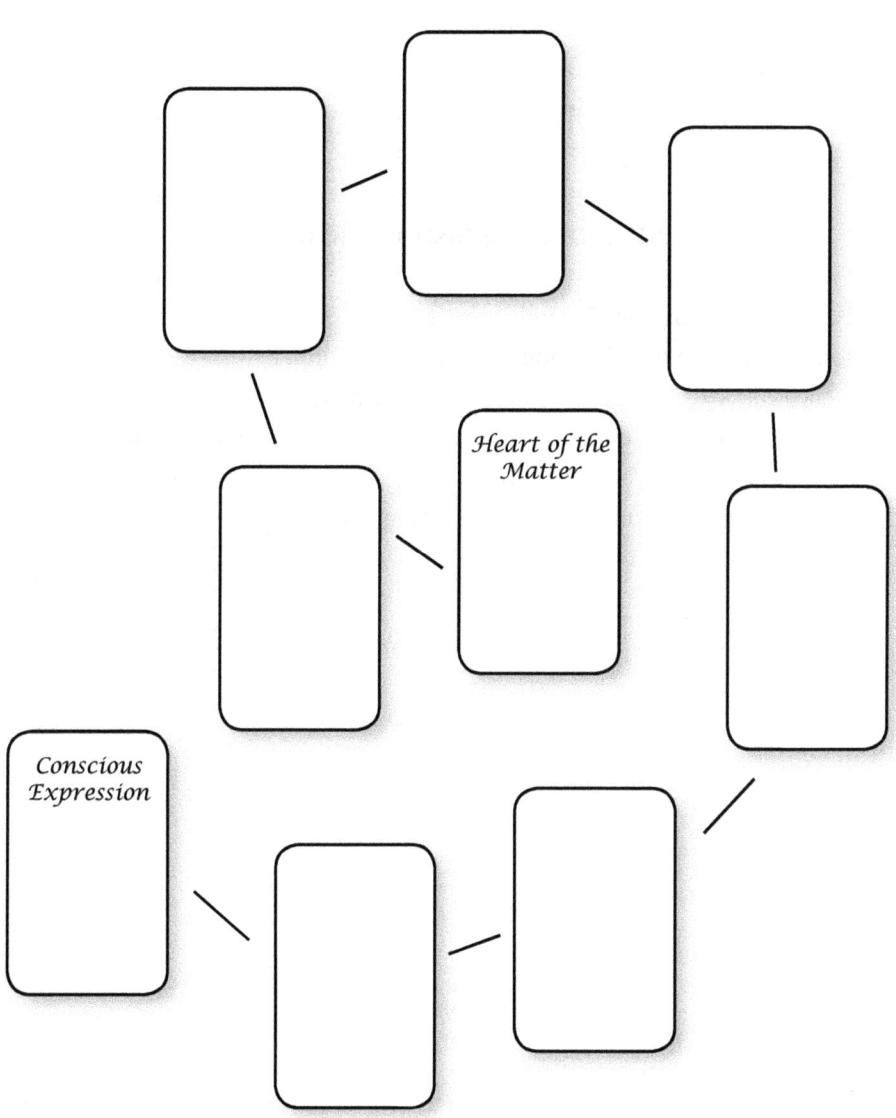

Created by Linda Farmer

Painting the Sistine Chapel

Painting the Sistine Chapel refers to your being inspired to create something lasting and meaningful; something impactful, regardless of what it is or of its size, that defines you and will remind you of your greatness. Separate the Major Arcana cards from the Minor Arcana and pick the Major Arcana card for position 6, first. Then shuffle both Arcanas together and pick the remaining cards. Make copies of the blank form for future use.

Painting the Sistine Chapel Spread
Lasting, Meaningful Creation

Question: Name
                                                      Date
                                                      Time
Feelings or Interpretations: Deck

7) How to use this power to achieve your desire

8) The gift that achieving your desire gives you

6) Major Arcana — The power that this knowledge gives you

5) What #3 and #4 reveal about you

3) Self-doubt

4) Self-confidence

2) What your desire really represents to you

1) Your desire

Created by Sheilaa Hite

What is My Life's Purpose?

The **What is My Life's Purpose?** spread is awesome. How many times have you asked yourself that question? My students and I were amazed at how accurately we could see ourselves and our paths. This spread is connected to the following spread, My Karma. Separate the Major Arcana cards from the Minor Arcana and pick the Major Arcana cards for positions 1, 4, 5, and 7 first. Then shuffle both Arcanas together and pick the remaining cards. Make copies of the blank form for future use.

What is My Life's Purpose? Spread

Question:

Feelings or Interpretations:

Name
Date
Time
Deck

1) Major Arcana
What is my life's purpose?

2) Minor Arcana
Am I fulfilling my life's purpose?

3) Minor Arcana
What do I need to do to fulfill my life's purpose?

4) Major Arcana
What are my hidden gifts/talents?

5) Major Arcana
What are my obvious gifts/talents?

6) Minor Arcana
How do I access and share my gifts and talents with the world?

7) Major Arcana
How is my karma connected to my life's purpose?

Created by Sheilaa Hite

My Karma

The **My Karma** spread is patterned after a set of scales with Major Arcana cards acting as the fulcrum that balances Fate and Destiny. It's a perfect mirror for seeing the results of the choices you make and the roads you're taking in life. Linked with the previous spread, What is My Life's Purpose?, it's remarkable in the way it reveals our personal truth to us. Separate the Major Arcana cards from the Minor Arcana and pick the Major Arcana cards for positions 1, 2, 3 and 4 first. Then shuffle both Arcanas together and pick the remaining cards. Make copies of the blank form for future use.

My Karma Spread

Question: Name
                                                 Date
                                                 Time
Feelings or Interpretations: Deck

1) Major Arcana
My Karma, Destiny or Fate. What I'm here to balance

2) Major Arcana
Divine Overview/ Guidance How do I balance my karma?

5) How settling for fate blocks, enslaves, weakens me

6) How creating my own destiny liberates, brings opportu-nities, empowers me

3) Major Arcana
How is my karma connected to my life's purpose?

7) Hidden, unconscious manifes-tations

8) Obvious manifes-tations

9) Hidden, subconscious manifes-tations

10) Conscious manifes-tations

4) Major Arcana
Foundation; main form or type of karmic issues

FATE
What you have to accept in life if you don't balance your karma. How you surrender your power. Your weaknesses.

DESTINY
What you can make of your life if you balance your karma. How you own & benefit from your power. Your strengths.

Created by Sheilaa Hite

Karma Crossroad

The **Karma Crossroad** spread gives us what we all want in life—a choice. It's so exciting to see that I can take a different path and what's likely to happen if I do. For such a 'heavy' topic, working with this spread created so much joy for my students and myself. In addition to answering the question at the top of the form, you can also ask about your karma with any person or situation. Separate the Major Arcana cards from the Minor Arcana and pick the Major Arcana cards for positions 1 and 7, first. Then shuffle both Arcanas together and pick the remaining cards. Make copies of the blank form for future use.

Karma Crossroad Spread

Question:

Feelings or Interpretations:

Name
Date
Time
Deck

4) Where this road leads

6) Where this road leads

3) What pattern will continue if I stay on this road

5) What new option/ freedom will emerge if I take this different road

2) Where I am now with my karma

7) Major Arcana

My perspective; My power; My how-to/ go-to

1) Major Arcana

What led me here

Created by Linda Farmer and Sheilaa Hite

About the Author

Sheilaa Hite, C.Ht., CLC, is a world renowned Master Tarot consultant, instructor, and Intuitive whose ability to expertly interpret and use the power and energy of the Tarot, as well as develop this gift in others, is legendary. She is featured in Paulette Cooper's book, "The 100 Top Psychics in America."

A naturally gifted Intuitive with an accuracy rate of 95-100%, she was born with the ability to 'see' and interpret information from the ethereal plane far beyond most in her field, bringing practical solutions to both spiritual and worldly issues. Her course—'The Tarot: A Counseling Tool for Psychologists'" makes excellent use of her skills as a teacher-diagnostician and has garnered high praise from the professionals who have consulted with her.

Acknowledged as "original," "charismatic" and "brilliantly insightful", she insightfully uses the Tarot, Astrology, Palmistry, Psychometry, Dream and Symbol Interpretation, Mediumship, Channeling, Meditation, Healing and Intuitive Counseling as she helps you understand and fulfill the meaning and purpose of your life. As one of the foremost life-skills mentors alive today, she is also a Certified Clinical Hypnotherapist, Past Life Regressionist, Certified Mentor/Life Coach, Healer, Motivational Speaker and Author.

Although she accepts the title of 'psychic' (because of the public's limited understanding of the Intuitive Arts), Sheilaa is an Intuitive because the power of her abilities stems from her highly developed intuition, which is directly connected to the source of all knowledge— The Creator. Through her powerful connection, she manifests Magic, Miracles and Joy for her clients and herself.

About the Author

As a media consultant, author and Intuitive, she has been featured on television in such programs as Entertainment Tonight, American Movie Classics, E! Television and NBC's groundbreaking, "The Other Side".

One of only a handful of people in the world permitted by the British government to enter and conduct ceremonies in the sacred 'inner circle of stones' in Stonehenge, she is also the first metaphysician authorized by the city of Malibu, California to teach in their facilities. As a Master of the Sacred Intuitive Arts, she naturally understands the true function of energy and knows how to powerfully work with it to help others influence their successful outcomes.

Her international client list numbers in the thousands and includes TV, movie and sports celebrities, politicians, homemakers, business professionals and members of the clergy and military. Her articles and columns have also appeared on-line, as well as in numerous national and international publications. Through her company, Odysseys—Grand Travel Experiences for the Heart, Spirit, Body and Mind—she also conducts tours and leads retreats to inspiring, beautiful places throughout the world.

As a catalyst of the soul and mind, her extraordinary ability to recognize, integrate and align the energies of the four creative realms have made her mastery at teaching others how to turn *"lead into gold,"* legendary. By synthesizing the expertise of her lifetime, extensive practical experience, sharp business acumen, innate intelligence and spot-on intuition, she uniquely unites and ignites the key elements that help guide her clients and students as they learn the modern-day alchemy secrets of making their dreams come true.

About the Author

*"I love my work, I love that I've been chosen to do it
and I love that I'm good at it.
Helping people to be happy and feel empowered makes me happy.
Life is a grand adventure and we are meant to enjoy and grow
from the experience."*

www.SheilaaHite.com

www.ingramcontent.com/pod-product-compliance
Lightning Source LLC
Chambersburg PA
CBHW062153080426
42734CB00010B/1665